The Secr
Subordinate That
EveryManager Should Know

A Success Handbook for Managers

by

William J. Crockett

First Edition

Center for Applied Behavioral Sciences
Sun City, Arizona

The Secrets of a Dynamic Subordinate That Every Manager Should Know

A Success Handbook for Managers

By William J. Crockett

Published by: **The Center for Applied Behavioral Sciences**

Post Office Box 1639

Sun City, AZ 85372 U.S.A.

Copyright © 1992 by Center for Applied Behavioral Sciences
First Printing 1992
Printed in the United States of America

Cover design by Robert Howard.
Printed by Patterson Printing Company

Library of Congress Cataloging in Publication Data
Crockett, William J.
The Secrets of a Dynamic Subordinate That Every Manager Should Know: A Success Handbook for Managers/by William J. Crockett.

CIP 92-070180
ISBN 0-9631995-5-5: $21.95 Softcover

ABOUT THE AUTHOR

For 21 years, Bill Crockett was with the United States Foreign Service and the State Department, serving in various cities—Naples, Rome, Beirut and Karachi.

From 1961 until January 1967, he was Deputy Under Secretary of State for Administration. He was initially appointed to that position by President Kennedy and continued in that capacity under President Johnson. As Deputy Secretary, Bill held the State Department's top management job, reporting directly to Secretary Dean Rusk. Responsibilities included: personnel, foreign service, budgets, security, passports and consular services, as well as management planning and development. It was during this time that Bill initiated an extensive organizational development program in the Department of State—one of the first such programs to be started in the Federal Government.

Bill retired from Government service in 1968 to join the World Trade Division of IBM. He then went to the Saga Corporation in Menlo Park, California, to become their Vice President for Human Resources. In this capacity, he designed and implemented an extensive program of organizational development for all levels of the company. While with the IBM World Trade Organization, the year prior to joining Saga, he developed a comprehensive executive development program.

Bill has had more than 50 articles published in the fields of management, motivation, and organizational development. His two favorites are his first one, "Team Building—One Approach to Organizational Development," and his last one, "Some Personal Payoffs of Team Building."

While in Government, Bill traveled extensively with President Johnson and worked closely with various committees of Congress on State Department matters.

President Johnson said of Bill: "On a personal note, I want you to know how reassuring it is to me, not only as President, but also as an American citizen, to have the caliber of public service which you give."

Bill Moyers, Special Assistant to the President, said: "Scores of people know how hard you worked to make the President's trip a success. Two of us, the President and myself, know better than any that it would not have been the same without you. You are one of those unique men who does a difficult job well without seeking credit. I will always be proud to have worked closely with you."

Carl Rowan wrote in one of his 1964 newspaper columns, "I know from first-hand experience that no single person in the State Department deserves as much credit as Crockett for the department's new attitude toward the employment and promotion of Negroes. When I joined State in 1961 I was the first and only Negro of deputy assistant secretary rank and the Department had only one Negro ambassador. Today a record six Negroes serve as ambassadors, the Department has three Negroes at deputy assistant secretary level, and the overall number of Negroes in key, high-level jobs has risen from 45 in 1961 to 142 today. Without Crockett's prodding and leadership, much of the progress just wouldn't have occurred."

And Mike Mansfield, while a Senator from Montana, made these remarks: "Mr. Crockett has found support as well as opposition in what he sought to do for the State Department in both the executive and legislative branches of the Government. But on matters of concern to both branches, he was ever patient, tolerant, and considerate, and in the end, immensely effective. There will be deep regret in the Congress as well as in the Administration, I am sure, from those who agreed or disagreed with Bill Crockett, that he has decided to leave the Government. The public service has lost a man of outstanding caliber and dedication."

To Write to the Author

We cannot guarantee that every letter written to the author can be answered, but all will be appreciated. Both the author and the publisher appreciate hearing from readers, learning of your enjoyment and benefit from this book. CABS also publishes a bimonthly "Human Relations Letter," and some readers' questions and comments to the author may be answered through its columns if permission to do so is included in the original letter. The author sometimes participates in seminars and workshops. To write to the author, or to ask a question, write to:

W. J. Crockett
CABS
P.O. Box 1639
Sun City, AZ 85372

Please enclose a self-addressed, stamped envelope for reply,
or $1.00 to cover costs.

ACKNOWLEDGMENT

I wish to thank all of the bosses I have had over the years, those unnamed as well as those named, who have provided the material for this book. It is my hope that others will learn from the tough lessons that I learned the hard way.

Without the dedicated and generous help of Marianne Brecher, this book could not have been written. Her typing and editing were enormously helpful.

I also wish to thank the former CEO of the Saga Corporation and my friend, Bill Scandling, for his suggestions and advice. The same can also be said for my son, Robert Crockett.

Lastly, I am enormously indebted to the former Chairman of the Saga Corporation and my friend, Bill Laughlin, for his encouragement and support in bringing the book to publication.

To all of these people, I proffer my most sincere thanks and appreciation.

W. J. Crockett

January 1992

FOREWORD

This book, "The Secrets of a Dynamic Subordinate That Every Manager Should Know," is about followership, the almost-forgotten element of life in all of our organizations, both public and private.

The world of organizations is composed of two roles, i.e., the leader/managers and the followers.

We give a great deal of attention to the management group. Hundreds of books have been written over the years on the theories of leadership/management. Our universities graduate hundreds of young people each year who have been trained to become leader/managers. Thousands of hours of management time and untold millions of dollars are spent each year in seminars and special courses teaching managers to manage. And still, many of our organizations, both public and private, are not highly successful, and the leadership/management failure rate is very high.

It seems to me, as it does to the author, that we have given very little thought or attention to the art of dynamic followership. I agree with the author when he says that leader/managers often fail because they have failed as followers and not necessarily because they are poor leader/managers. Dissatisfied bosses fire subordinates; subordinates don't fire their managers!

It is of vital importance that our leader/managers come to recognize that one of the most overlooked elements of their job (and yet the one that is critically important to their success) is their followership skill — their ability to create strong, positive relationships with their bosses. This book carries that powerful message to managers at all levels. It is indeed a manager's handbook for success.

I urge all leader/managers at all levels in all organizations to use this book as the basis for the training of subordinates in the art of followership. But most of all, I urge all leader/managers to use this book as a handbook for their own success.

Good luck.

W. P. Laughlin
One of the Three Founders and Former Chairman of the Board
The Saga Corporation

HOW THIS BOOK CAN HELP YOU TO SUCCEED

This book will help you to succeed in your job. It will enhance your career. It will help you to create positive relationships with the most important people in your work-lives—your bosses.

This book is unique in the annals of management literature in that it looks up the chain of command and addresses the leader/manager's relationship with his/her boss. While the quality of this relationship may not be the key to the productivity and success of the organization, it definitely is the key to how long a leader/manager will remain with the organization. Our failure to please our boss, no matter what our level in the organization, will mean that we may be moved, demoted, or discharged.

A headline in the Tuesday, Nov. 26, 1991 "Wall Street Journal" shouts:

"IBM Shunts Aside Conrades Thought to Have Been Contender for Chairman." The story goes on to tell how his fellow IBM'ers feel that Conrades was "clearly demoted." The story also discloses the harsh way in which the announcement was made, as if his boss, Chairman John F. Akers, was deliberately trying to humiliate him, thereby sending a tough message to all IBM managers. Other stories suggested that he may have also been "too hot" a contender for his boss's job. Whatever the real reason for his demotion, the lesson is again made clear: A subordinate at any level in an organization, even a senior vice president like Mr. Conrades, must fulfill the needs of his/her boss in order for him/her to succeed.

Another example concerns President Bush and his then Chief of Staff, Governor Sununu. The story tells how the press criticized Mr. Sununu for a statement that the President had made in a recent speech. In frustration and anger, Mr. Sununu flared:

"I did not put that into the President's speech. He ad-libbed it."

Mr. Sununu's need, whatever it was, took priority in his behavior over the best interests of his boss, President Bush. This is a very good way to get one's self fired. (Mr. Sununu subsequently resigned.)

This book is what is called "a book of experience-based theory." The concepts are gleaned from the author's experience of being a leader/manager for more than 50 years and having the task of pleasing a boss every one of those years! Together with the material in the appendix, this book will help you to understand a little better how to meet the challenge of maintaining a strong positive relationship with your boss.

TABLE OF CONTENTS

Introduction   **11**

Chapter I • Appreciating the Duality
               of the Leadership Role   **15**

The Keystone Qualities:

Chapter II • Loyalty   **23**

Chapter III • Honesty   **31**

Chapter IV • Performance   **41**

Chapter V • Personality   **59**

The Basic Attitudes:

Chapter VI • Accepting that the boss
                 owns the job   **65**
                 A. What   **66**
                 B. When   **69**
                 C. How   **75**

Chapter VII • Trust
                  A. Building Trust   **79**
                  B. The Source of Power   **91**
                  C. The Source of Autonomy   **101**

We Make It Happen:

Chapter VIII   **107**

Conclusion   **121**

Appendix
   Understanding Human Nature   **125**
   Index   **201**

Order Form   **203**

INTRODUCTION

The world is filled with subordinates. There are millions upon millions of us. We are of every race, every color, every sex, and every age. We are at every level in organizations, from CEO to hourly worker. We exist in every nation, regardless of its economic system or its political persuasion. We subordinates are like the poor — we populate the earth! And each of us has a boss who holds a good deal of power over us. It is that boss who is our own source of security and power. We have earned both when, in his eyes, we have become trustworthy and effective subordinates.

Although Daniel Webster neglected to include the word "subordinancy" in the dictionary, I define subordinancy as being a relationship where one person, called the subordinate, is controlled by the authority of another person, called the superior, or in more mundane terms, the boss.

In this book the word "subordinate" refers to a very select and discrete group of subordinates, i.e., those who have risen to the rank of leader-manager.

To some people, the word "subordinancy" carries an image of low status and authority——an image almost like subservience. When I told a high-level manager that this book is about subordinancy, he said with some disdain, "I might buy it for my secretary to read, but I would never buy it for myself." The anomaly of this declaration is that he is fully as much of a subordinate as is his secretary, and conceivably, since he is a manager, he might need the information contained in the book even more! The word "subordinate" is not a description of a rank in an organizational hierarchy; it refers to the vertical relationship that exists between people in all organizations from the top to the bottom. The president of an organization is as much a subordinate in his relationship to his board of directors as is the supervisor of the cleaning crew in his relationship to his boss.

The substantive and managerial work that each subordinate does and the responsibility that each carries are enormously different, but the relationship that they have to their respective bosses is made up of the very same basic components. This book deals with those components.

Hundreds, if not thousands, of books have been written over the years on the subjects of leadership and management. New ones appear every year, each touting a new theory on how leaders-managers can do their jobs more effectively. All management books look down the organizational chain of command and address the leadership concerns of managers at all levels in the organization. The world of leadership-managers is absolutely mesmerized by the question, "How can we lead-manage our people and our organization so that they will become more efficient and effective?"

The result of this obsession with making leadership-management the primary agent for organizational effectiveness is that most of our formal academic teaching, most of our corporate-sponsored seminars, and most of the manpower-development programs within our organizations are devoted to the subject of improving management and leadership skills. Leadership has become the single theme of our countless efforts to develop people who can make our organizations vital and productive. Leadership has become the illusive, miracle quality that we seek to develop in people. To be sure, as we look at the world scene and contemplate the situation facing both business and government, it does indeed seem that effective, capable and creditable leadership is in a state of chronic short supply! We do need leaders—leaders who feel and exercise a strong sense of positive power over the people who report to them, thereby galvanizing the whole organization into achieving great goals. Mrs. Thatcher did this for England when she was Prime Minister.

More to the point, however, is the fact that the best leaders-managers in the world of organizations will not for long remain leaders-managers unless they also are dynamic subordinates—unless they satisfy their bosses. Again, we have Margaret Thatcher as an example of this immutable law of human affairs, i.e. even the most capable leaders must keep their power base—their bosses—satisfied! As great as our leadership-management need may be, our greater need is for our leaders-managers to learn how they can become more effective in their relationships with their bosses. This concept is what this book deals with.

There are some terms that we should agree on before we go further.

First, there are the "superiors" in the workplace. Who are they? They are the bosses, the leaders, the supervisors, the foremen, and the managers. They are all the other not-so-diplomatic phrases that we sometimes use to designate those persons for whom we work who hold direct power and authority over us, no matter how high we may rise in the organization. They are the ones who are responsible for insuring that we do our jobs and that we achieve the goals and objectives that have been set for us. These are the people who judge us, reward us, and, when circumstances require, punish us. As long as we work, we will always be under the direct authority and watchful eye of a boss!

Second, there is "us"—the subordinates at all managerial and supervisory levels in the organization. We are managers, leaders, supervisors, foremen and staff who fill the dual role of being subordinates to our bosses and bosses to our subordinates. We are the group this book is directed toward.

What is "dynamic"? "Dynamic" is our enthusiasm, our positive attitude and our turned-on behavior that transcends the humdrum and puts us into high gear for doing our present tasks. It is our motivation to achieve. Most important, perhaps, this sense of motivation flows from a dynamic subordinate's own feelings of power and self-esteem. We are not dependent upon having a dynamic leader-manager for us to be dynamic. We are self-motivators.

"Dynamic" means our ability to take charge of and take control over the situations in which we find ourselves. It means that we will decide what we will do and not do, take and not take from our boss and our work. It means that whether we will leave a particular situation or not will be our decision, and it is our decision as to what we must do for and with ourselves in order to achieve the goals that we set for ourselves.

This book is not a book of theory. It recounts my own experience over 50 years of being a leader-manager/subordinate, and the important lessons that I learned along the way. One can disagree with theory and can readily discard it as not being workable in the reality of one's own work-world. The concepts that I describe and illustrate in this book cannot be discarded as being irrelevant; they have worked for me, and they may also work for you.

For example, I learned that the four criteria for a successful leader-manager are loyalty, honesty, performance and personality. Chapters II-V of the book deal with these four keystone concepts. The person who masters and practices these four principles has a virtual lock on success.

The next two chapters deal with the two key attitudes—beliefs—
that a leader-manager must adhere to in order to insure his success.
These are: Our boss owns our job; and Job certainty is the basis of
power.

The two final chapters deal with trust and the autonomy that flows
to the leader-manager who fulfills all of these criteria. Whether or not
you will accept the challenge to fulfill these criteria is up to you. No one
can do it for you.

It was my privilege to be associated with the great psychologist,
Abraham Maslow, during the last years of his life. Once when I was
bemoaning my lack of psychological education, he said to me, "Bill,
stop your moaning and look to your own experiences for learnings
about people. Most of us professionals have learned what we know by
our study of rats. You may not know the fancy words or understand
the theories of professional psychologists, but you have in your own
guts the reality of life and relationships. So don't moan. Start looking
inward and become an acting psychologist who can help people to
understand the essence of relationships in a practical way."

I hope that you, too, will dig deeply into your own experiences and
awareness and uncover the messages and the treasures now hidden
there on how to relate to the power figures that fill your work life. *That*
is the source of your own successful leadership.

Good luck,

Bill Crockett

Chapter One

Appreciating the Duality of the Leadership Role

"The Child is Father of the Man"

A poet once wrote, "The child is father of the man...," and in the same context the subordinate is the father of the manager. The very qualities that a boss most values in a subordinate are the qualities that he must exercise with his own boss if he is to be successful. Therefore, leaders-managers at all levels in an organization must understand and embrace the fact they are subordinates in one role and that they will forever be subordinates no matter how high they rise in the organization. Furthermore, they must forever commit themselves to the primacy of this subordinate role. They must behave in ways that make their bosses fully trust them as subordinates.

I have friends who once lived with a miniature French Poodle named Fifi. She had a delightful personality—friendly, smart, vivacious, playful, and sometimes naughty. She was one of the family. She ate with them, slept with them and went places with them. They rarely acknowledged that she was a dog, and of course they never said "that word" in her presence. They were part of a conspiracy that helped her to think of herself as being a human.

Fifi was spoiled, and on the rare occasions when she was left at home alone, she would do something naughty to show her displeasure—strew toilet paper all over the house, scatter newspapers, or if terribly angry, maybe shred a curtain. At these times she might be treated like a dog; but these times were far and few between so she mostly behaved as if she thought of herself as being human—all human.

Then one day when she was in the yard with her friend and owner, a fierce Doberman came bounding onto the scene, having escaped from his master. Fifi, oblivious as usual to the fact that she was only a dog, flew at the monster in a raucous rage and, in a single snap and crunch, Fifi's life was gone. Fifi had confused the dual nature of her role, sometimes dog and sometimes human, and acted in the wrong role; as a consequence she died.

We, like Fifi, often forget the dual nature of the roles that we play in our work lives. Except for a very few of us, we are and forever will be cast in the dual role of leader-manager/subordinate. But, like Fifi, we often forget the requirements and perhaps, at times, even the existence of our subordinancy role, and consequently we run the risk of being hurt.

The dual nature of the subordinate/leader-manager role can be illustrated by a vertical line that points upward and downward from a middle starting point "A". It looks like this:

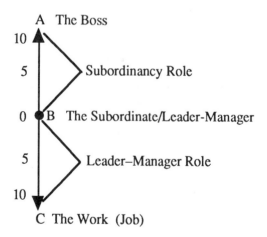

The person's "leader-manager" role is plotted on the line B-C and his "subordinate" role on line A-B. The person, of course, is responsible for fulfilling the requirements of the whole line—A to C.

In the "leader-manager" role, the person is the boss. Ofttimes his full attention is directed downward to getting the job done. He establishes goals, organizes the work, sets schedules, plans strategies, makes decisions, directs people and causes action to take place. It is an absorbing, time-consuming, challenging and exhilarating role. The person at "B" holds great power over people and situations. In many cases, he carries heavy substantive responsibilities for achieving organizational success. He may exercise such a single-minded drive to achieve or to exceed his work goals (C) that he works many extra hours each week, often taking work home to be done in the evening and on Saturday and Sunday. Achieving his work goals may become such a driving force in his life that he loses sight of his other people-responsibilities, including his wife, his children, and his boss. He not only forgets the importance of his upward relationships (A-B), but by the way that he works, he has little time to function in his subordinancy role. Most such people make the erroneous assumption that as long as the work itself is being done well, the other part of the job (A-B) doesn't really matter—"it will take care of itself."

The boss himself may play a subtle and even malicious part in this subordinate's behavior by doing simultaneously two contradictory things. First, the boss may put such great importance on the subordinate's attaining the work goals that he becomes the direct cause of the subordinate's one-track work-method. He, in fact, may have forced the subordinate's one-sided concept of his schedule. By his own failure to involve himself with the subordinate other than taking an interest in the work, he is erroneously sending messages to the subordinate that he doesn't value or need the subordinate's upward relationship with him. The end is that all too often the subordinate is seduced into a false sense of both power and security.

There are classic examples where well-known and important leaders-managers have been fired because they did not recognize the importance of their subordinancy roles. It might well be that they were so anxious about their work and so occupied with their leader-managerial roles that they had no time to do anything about their upward relationships. Both Lee Iaccoca and General Douglas MacArthur are examples of high achievers (scale B-C) who failed. Despite their well-known records of achievement in their work (B-C), they were both fired by their bosses. Why? Why would men with such impressive records of success be fired? Why? The answer is easy: neither had bothered to develop positive and trusting upward relationships with their bosses (A-B). They had failed to recognize or to heed the most basic of all leadership-management concepts, i.e., the essence of leadership is being a dynamic subordinate (line A-B).

It is the wise leader-manager who realizes early in his career that his most complete success will be achieved only to the extent that he can move both his work line (B-C) and his relationship line (A-B) as close to the magic 10/10 rating as possible.

I have personally known cases where managers have done their work so well and handled their relationships so poorly that they were rated a 10 on their work and a 0 on their relationhips. And then, when they failed, they were unable to accept or to understand the reasons! "I did my job well!"

It is almost beyond comprehension that so many managers in today's world conceive of their jobs as being in only one dimension—their work—and fail to give any attention to their relationships. Any subordinate who conducts himself in this manner puts himself in great jeopardy. Ultimately he probably will fail.

To restate what would seem to be the obvious, more people get into trouble with their bosses and finally get fired because they have failed in their subordinancy role (maintaining strong upward relationships) than because they have failed in their leadership-management role. In these cases, they have failed to develop strong and trusting relationships with their bosses. They didn't, in their subordinancy role, fulfill their bosses' needs—whatever they may have been. The old cliche which says, "I am nervous when I have a nervous boss, especially if he is nervous because of me!," is a reality in the workplace.

The Wall Street Journal of August 23, 1990, carried an article that uniquely illustrates this concept. According to this article, the president of CBS News, despite his success in rejuvenating the network's coverage, faced imminent ouster because of his failure to establish a positive relationship with his boss. When a manager at any level fails to recognize the potency and critical nature of his subordinancy role, he will soon be in deep trouble.

It is the number-one responsibility of all subordinates to insure that a strong, trusting relationship exists between his boss and himself.

While many subordinates refer to their supervisors as "the boss," and while they know that "the boss" exercises power over them, most of the time they still don't feel like subordinates. They feel like leaders-managers. Just as Fifi forgot that she was a dog, most leaders-managers, at all levels of the hierarchy, often forget that they also are subordinates. They give their major attention and energy to making sure that they succeed at their "jobs."

I have no hard data that will shed light on the reasons for this phenomenon. From my own experience in both the role of boss and the role of subordinate, it is my belief that this over-developed, lopsided sense of being a leader-manager (giving most of one's attention to the "job") occurs for six main reasons:

• Many people, especially at the upper levels, are hired into the organization as leaders-managers. This aspect of their role is the only thing that is discussed in the hiring process. Their experience, training and success in fulfilling this leadership-managerial role is emphasized. Their subordinancy skills are never questioned. The relationship requirements and responsibilities of the job are not mentioned.

• Most people who come out of our business colleges and universities come with an impressive array of management-oriented credentials. It is safe to say that they have learned little or nothing about being effective subordinates. They aren't hired as subordinates and they don't feel like subordinates. They feel like leaders/managers and, as a result, they act out their feeling orientation, i.e., as managers.

• The careers of leaders-managers in most organizations—government, business, and military—are usually liberally sprinkled with "Management Development" and "Leadership Training" opportunities. They spend many weeks of their professional lives in posh hotel training-centers learning the principles, theories, and skills of leadership-management. Little if any of this training is ever directed to the leaders'-managers' need to create positive upward relationships. This whole setting and learning process contributes to people perceiving themselves only as leaders-managers.

• The leaders'-managers' daily tasks emphasize the nature of their leadership-managerial roles. They make plans, help to organize the work, participate in making important decisions, make high-level presentations, attend impressive functions, lead (manage) their own teams of subordinates, and meet with important others. This is all heady stuff. Even bosses join this unstated conspiracy to cause their subordinates to think only of their management tasks by referring to them as "my management team," or "my senior managers," and so on. Like Fifi, subordinates soon forget that they are subordinates!

• Our modern results-oriented philosophy also helps to muffle our role as subordinates. As leaders-managers, we are required to share with our bosses our plans for getting and keeping our team's performance on track; we are required to make periodic reports to our boss on our progress; and we are required to explain the reasons for problems that develop. All of this is frequently carried on in the clinical atmosphere of hard-data facts, figures, plans, actions and results—nothing in the encounter jars our self-image as leaders-managers!

Even more important, the boss' need for his subordinate to behave and relate to him in ways that will create trust and support are never discussed. These needs are not made a part of the goal that the subordinate/leader-manager must achieve. The subordinancy role is left unmentioned as if it is so self-evident that it needs no discussion. Of course, we all know that this is not the case.

• Finally, the higher a person rises in the organizational world the less he may feel like a subordinate. Leaders-managers are given fancy titles, plush offices, impressive perks, big salaries and awesome responsibilities. They have power over people and situations. They rub elbows with other powerful figures who fan their egos. On the other hand, many of the people with whom they deal are often obsequious as well as respectful.

When this happens, people can easily start feeling their own importance. It is truly hard for some people in such circumstances to feel like a subordinate let alone act like one! In such cases the person might start thinking (believing) "it is all mine—I really own this job." Powerful public figures like Keating, Milken, Poindexter, North and others may have had such feelings. It is very human for us to feel this way when we reach the highest positions of power, influence, and prestige. "The Keating Five," when they bashed the well-deserving bureaucracy, no doubt felt that they were doing what they had a right to do from their position of power. Power does indeed corrupt the judgment and perception of whose who hold it. Subordinate? Who me? Subordinate to whom?

Yet in their private worlds, powerful leaders-managers may sometimes mutter a few choice words in describing that so-and-so—the boss, thus revealing the fact that they have some awareness and perhaps even uneasiness about their position. In the security of darkness and their bed, they may share with their spouse some anxieties they feel in their subordinate role; but most of the time Fifi's tragic charade persists: "I am not really a subordinate, I am a leader-manager."

The powerful negative emotional forces that can arise when a strong-minded boss is ignored by an equally strong-minded and aggressive subordinate are often not recognized or are ignored and pushed into the background by the subordinate. As time goes on, these negative feelings may become stronger and stronger in the boss. As a result, one day the boss may become so angry, so frustrated, and so fed up with the subordinate's attitude and behavior that he explodes, with the result being that the subordinate may be fired. Then the subordinate who thought of himself only as a leader-manager comes face to face with the reality of his dual role. He was primarily a subordinate after all with all the attendant vulnerabilities! Iaccoca and MacArthur both tasted the bitter truth of their own subordinancy!

On the other hand, rich rewards await the subordinate who by his awareness of his dual role moves his work and his relationships to be close to the 10/10 on the subordinancy and leader-manager scales. This means, of course, that the person not only does his job well but that he also has created a positive and trusting relationship with his boss.

CONCLUSION:
It may well be that it is in the performance of our leadership-management roles that we gain most of our own personal fulfillment and satisfaction in our work. We no doubt enjoy the power that we exercise in making our leadership-management roles effective. But we must be ever mindful that the source of our power is our boss! If we lose his trust, we stand to lose all.

The key to our success in dealing with the complex human world of bosses is for us to make sure that we perceive the dual nature of our roles in proper perspective—we are first and foremost a subordinate and then, and then only are we leader-managers! We must make sure that our boss is fully aware that this is our perspective as evidenced by our ongoing, day-in and day-out behavior in relating to him. We must make our concept obvious to him.

It is the purpose of this book to help subordinates understand the absolute necessity for making sure that in their drive for success, they have not overlooked the awful consequences of failure to build and maintain a positive relationship with their bosses.

Dobermans run rampant in organizations looking for those, like Fifi, who have allowed their perception of who they are to become distorted!

We who are cast in the dual role of leader manager/subordinate have a golden opportunity to learn by first-hand experience in managing our own subordinates what is required of us in attitude and behavior in order for us to be successful and dynamic subordinates. While we are acting as leaders-managers, we can take note of the things that we want our subordinates to do and refrain from doing. We can discover in our own guts the attitudes, the behavior, and the skills that our subordinates use with us that make us feel secure, that help us to feel that the organization is ours, and that we have a place in it, that we do have power, and that we can feel good about ourselves in our management roles. We can also learn the things that subordinates do or do not do that create trust as well as things that destroy it. We must learn to use these skills and attitudes when we are dealing with our own bosses.

This is one of the secrets of dynamic subordinancy.

Chapter Two

Loyalty—the First Keystone Quality

"A Deep Sense of Loyalty Gives a Man Personal Meaning and Integrity"

The first success secret of any dynamic subordinate is his personal commitment of absolute loyalty to his boss. This is the case whether or not it is actively and overtly mandated by a boss; but there are situations where a boss directly makes this a condition of continued employment.

When I was nominated by President Kennedy to become the Assistant Secretary of State for Administration, I was called to the office of the U.S. Attorney General for a briefing/interview. At that time, the President's brother, Mr. Robert Kennedy, was the Attorney General. The meeting went like this:

I arrived at the appointed time and was told by Mr. Kennedy's secretary to go on in. I hesitated at the door because one of the largest dogs that I had ever seen lay across the doorway. I glanced in and saw Mr. Kennedy, a small man, sitting in the far corner of a huge room at a huge desk. He sensed my presence and without looking up said, "Step over him!" I did carefully step over the dog and went across the room to his desk and, at his nod, sat in a side chair by his desk.

He said, "Do you know what your job is at the State Department?" Since I was a career officer in the Foreign Service with some fifteen years of experience, I thought that I knew something of what the job should be; but he gave me no chance to answer. He said, "Your job is to make the Department of State responsive to the will of my brother, the President. He will make the foreign policy and your State Department colleagues will carry it out. Your job is to make them loyal to the President. Do you understand?"

"Yes, Sir," I replied.

Then, "Do you know how to do your job?" he asked. I thought that I did, but I sensed that he would also tell me, which he did:

"The way for your to get this job done is by kicking everyone in the ass so hard that the teeth will rattle in every consulate all around the world! Do you understand?"

"Yes, Sir," I replied.

Then he said, "I don't know how you got appointed to this job, but make no mistake about where your own loyalties lie. You may travel with Rooney and report to Rusk, but you will be loyal only to my brother, the President. Do you understand?"

"Yes, Sir," I replied. And that ended the interview.

Loyalty was put high on the list of the priorities that the President (and his brother) held for his subordinates.

This vow of absolute loyalty is the first requirement for the success and survival of any subordinate at any level in any organization. Whether or not it is overtly mandated by a boss, the wise subordinate knows that it is his own highest priority to fill!

The concept of loyalty has many meanings.

• Support is a meaning of loyalty that is always appropriate. In days of crisis when things are going badly for the boss, support is appreciated. Then, if ever, the boss needs our total support.

We must not only obey the legal demands of our bosses, but we must support him in all the decisions that he makes, whether or not we agree with them. Our job is to protect the boss from mistakes and problems, not finger him for criticism by the press and others.

President Kennedy's decision to help the Cubans who were in the United States as refugees to invade Castro's Cuba in 1964 was a disaster. Of course there was a public clamor with lots of accusatory questions. Chester Bowles, then Under Secretary of State under Dean Rusk, slipped word to the press: "I was against doing it but I was overruled!" This really hit the fan and not too long thereafter, Mr. Bowles was no longer a member of the presidential councils! He was "promoted" to an overseas post as Ambassador. Self-preservation at the expense of our bosses is one form of blatant disloyalty that bosses won't tolerate.

Sometimes loyalty may be more of a perception than a fact. It may only be how we are perceived by our bosses in our relationship with his enemies. If we are seen as being too cozy with them, our boss will quite naturally (he, too, is human) assume that we may be disloyal.

- "Taking the heat" is another function of loyalty.

President Johnson had a fetish about this kind of loyalty. When I was Deputy Under Secretary of State, the President sometimes called me directly, as he did others. That special white telephone which connected me with the President of the United States jangled authoritatively on my desk late one Friday afternoon. I knew from experience that it would mean trouble of some kind, for no other kind of message ever came to me from my boss, President LBJ!

After the warm-up formalities——expressions of how much he needed me, trusted me and liked me——came his order:

"Bill, you have a fellow who works for you who is very disloyal to me personally and to my whole administration. I want you to get rid of him. I don't want him around any longer. He is a bad apple in our barrel. He is not on our team, and he is causing me a lot of trouble on the Hill with the liberals. So fire him, Bill, and the faster the better!"

"I presume that you are speaking of the Administrator of Security and Consular Affairs, Mr. President?"

"Don't be coy with me, Bill, you know damned well who I am talking about!"

"Okay, Mr. President, but I don't have any real cause to fire him. He was actually very instrumental in getting our immigration legislation passed. I don't think it is really fair for me to fire him, Mr. President."

A forbidding silence followed, and I knew that I must come up with something, so I said, "Mr. President, as you know, we have already streamlined the Bureau of Administration by eliminating the job of Assistant Secretary of State for Administration. This is the equivalent of the job of Administrator for Security and Consular Affairs. You also are aware that we are about ready to submit another reorganization plan to Congress that would eliminate the job of Administrator of Security and Consular Affairs. The Administrator is out of the country right now, so we have held up taking it to the Hill until he returns. I want to talk to him about it before we actually take it to the Hill. So — when that plan of reorganization is approved, the man that you want fired, the incumbent, will be without a job. I had thought that we would offer him an ambassadorship someplace, which he might or might not take. Would that be an okay solution for you?"

After a moment's silence, the President said, "Yes, that sounds okay to me, Bill. And let's hope that the ambassadorship that you offer him will be a hell of a long distance from Washington! And Bill, you alone will have to take the political heat from this one and there may be a lot. He has a lot of friends! I talked to Rusk about it and he said to talk to you. So when the heat comes, as it surely will, neither Rusk nor I will publicly support you. So do it well and wish for luck! I'm glad you are on my team, Bill! And good luck."

I heard from him no more on this issue.

Our reorganization plans had somehow gotten leaked to the Administrator's staff. They, of course, couldn't wait to tell him about it when they met him at the plane upon his return from abroad. When he heard the news, he announced his resignation on the spot, without discussing the matter with me.

In one way his resignation made my job easy. I have never seen or heard from him directly since, but I heard a lot from him indirectly via his friends in Congress and in other high places. Subsequently I took a lot of heat on this, but in time the issue was swallowed up and forgotten by the emergence of hotter and more significant matters.

• Another form of loyalty is that of making our differences with our boss' policies and decisions known to him. This is a tricky, ticklish business that must be very carefully handled by the subordinate.

Most bosses don't like subservience and don't trust "yes" people. Most bosses want subordinates who will challenge their ideas, differ with their decisions, give them data, put forward new ideas for doing things, and who will dare to be uniquely themselves. *But*—in order to implement this kind of behavior the subordinate must come from a base of absolute trust and not from a role of competitive counterdependency. To succeed at this important role, a subordinate must have demonstrated his absolute personal loyalty to the boss in many other situations.

The role of loyal opposition or devil's advocate is an important one for all subordinates to play. However, they must learn to come across as caring rather than punishing, probing rather than judging, collaborative rather than competitive—and in all events, above all else, loyal.

I was Deputy Under Secretary of State under Dean Rusk during our military involvement in Vietnam. President Johnson was harassed on all fronts by people and groups who did not approve of our efforts there. As a result, the President put a high value on loyalty—loyalty to him and to the government's position. If you disagreed with any decision, you ran the risk of being punished for being disloyal. And many were punished severely.

There was one man in the high echelons of government who played the role of devil's advocate, loyal opposition, and survived. He not only survived but he was cited by President Johnson as "my loyal friend, George Ball, who shares with me his doubts while supporting our course of action." At the time, George Ball was Under Secretary of State, Dean Rusk's deputy. And while all of Mr. Ball's publicly-expressed doubts and concerns did not change the President's thinking on the course of government policy, still it served a useful purpose. It can be done if it is based on absolute loyalty.

By our actions, our words and our attitude, we must not let anyone come to believe that we are competing with our chief for anything—for credit, for glory, for status, for power, for publicity, etc. This is a dangerous game that some subordinates have tried to play, always with disastrous results.

• Another form of loyalty is taking risks for our boss.

People in high places are often severely harassed by people seeking answers and problems seeking solutions. They are so beset by these pressures that they become emotionally exhausted. The wise and sensitive subordinate will become aware of these situations when they occur and will cause two things to happen. First, they will help to deny access to their boss from people who have problems; and second, they will take the risk of solving some of these problems themselves.

This was dramatically illustrated to me when I traveled abroad with Vice President Johnson. The days and nights were packed with meetings, interviews, VIP's, dinners and speeches. Yet I, as the person responsible for the daily schedule, felt that I must see the Vice President. There was no way that I could make decisions for him. I didn't have the experience, nor did I have his trust. But there was a person with us who had both.

In those days, Bill Moyers was on the staff of Vice President Johnson. Bill was positive, loyal, and highly trusted by LBJ. Bill was fully aware of LBJ's need to be personally involved in almost all decisions about the schedule, and he also was keenly aware of the physical and emotional strain that the trip was putting on the Vice President. So Bill fearlessly and responsibly risked for the Vice President. I would go directly to Bill with my problems and questions which, under normal conditions, I would take up directly with Mr. Johnson. Bill then would make the decisions——not in a self-aggrandizing manner which puffed his own importance, but in a thoughtful, considerate, self-effacing manner that gave evidence of the fact that Bill was indeed thinking only of the best interest of his boss.

Once the decisions were made, Bill stood behind them. If Mr. Johnson looked upon a decision critically, Bill took the heat. Bill took risks for his boss.

• An important type of loyalty is behaving in ways that don't embroil the boss in public controversy.

There are some kinds of behavior that might at first seem to be dynamic but are neither dynamic nor loyal. For example, a dynamic subordinate is not a subordinate who takes off on a wild tangent or sets up new targets for action that have a questionable legality without consulting his boss, like a North or Poindexter in the Reagan White House. That behavior is delinquent, not dynamic, and inevitably brings public discredit on the boss' ability to manage.

"Dynamic" is not a subordinate who helps his boss cover up a shady deal, like a Halderman or Erhlichmann in the Nixon Administration. That is being subservient and conspiratorial, and helps no one who is involved.

Nor is "dynamic" a subordinate who assiduously tries to gather the boss' power to himself so that he becomes the reality and the boss becomes the shadow, like a Regan, who was Reagan's chief of staff. That is disloyalty at its ugliest.

The public controversy and embarrassment that Chief of Staff John Sununu brought to President Bush not only was poor judgment but smacks of disloyalty as well.

• A loyal subordinate does not badmouth his boss.

When I was a young man in high school, I worked for a very bad boss in a grocery store. He was irascible, unappreciative and dictatorial. I had an older colleague who called him "old pain-in-the-ass" because we suspected that he had hemorrhoids.

Every time this colleague and I were alone doing something together, this colleague would talk about "old pain-in-the-ass." "Old pain-in-the-ass" did this, said that, etc. etc. One day the inevitable happened——"old pain-in-the-ass" was on the other side of a pile of grocery boxes and heard us! I can still remember my embarrassment, my shame, my guilt and my fear when he appeared to confront us.

He said to my colleague, "Jim, you are old enough to know better than to do what you are doing! You can go home right now and take the rest of the week off without pay. And this is your final warning! I want you to look up and bring to me next Monday morning a copy of the Elbert Hubbard quotation about being a loyal subordinate. And as for you, Bill, I will not punish you, but I hope that you have learned a lifelong lesson. No matter who the boss is or what he does, as long as you work for him you owe him your absolute loyalty. Now let's all get back to work!"

And for sure, I have never forgotten that lesson!

CONCLUSION:

Loyalty to another is a hard task for people because it calls for attitudes and actions that at first glance seem to be contrary to the subordinate's own self-interest. Thus it is that the higher in the organization we progress, the more difficult it is for us to maintain our upward loyalty. Our own needs for recognition, power and autonomy become so powerful that it is indeed hard for us to retain the attitudes and do the things that will demonstrate our loyalty to our bosses.

But——it is the wise subordinate who controls his own needs so that he can in reality be and become a loyal subordinate in all of its meanings. It is the win/win way to go because it sows the seeds of trust which are so vital to the success of the subordinate.

Chapter Three

Honesty—The Second Keystone Quality

"Honesty is not only the best policy—it is the only policy that will bring trusting relationships."

The second success secret of a dynamic subordinate is his personal honesty. It is quite easy for us to glibly say, "Why of course I am honest. I wouldn't lie and I wouldn't take anything that didn't belong to me!" This is indeed one aspect of honesty; but there are other important dimensions in an honest relationship that we must be aware of. These are:

• Honesty is fully revealing the condition of the job. This means that we make sure that our boss knows about the things that are going wrong as well as the things that are going right. It means not withholding bad news.

Of course there are surprises in all walks of life—things going wrong, like the grounding of the Exxon Valdez. If the tide starts to turn for the worse in any of our activities—in the areas of operations, profits, negotiations, etc.—we must immediately tell the boss what is going on and why, and what we plan to do about it. It is critical that the boss be informed at once. In the case of the Valdez, it was several hours before the captain notified the Coast Guard of his problem—too late to get effective help.

Telling the boss what's going on with us serves to make the boss our advocate. The only viable relationship between a subordinate and his boss is that of trust and collaboration. Telling the boss about our jobs gives him the data to discuss with others what is happening in his area. And it fortifies him and prepares him to better handle the complaints about us that are sure to come to him from those who disagree with us and the way we do our jobs.

A colleague of mine once advised me, "Why tell the old man the bad news? If he doesn't hear it we won't get bawled out. If he does hear it and we haven't told him, we'll only get bawled out once. Not telling him the bad news will reduce our trouble with him by at least one-half!" That is a dishonest basis on which to try to build a trusting relationship, and it can only result in suspicion, guilt and mistrust.

When the boss knows that we are absolutely honest about the conditions of our work, his trust will build.

• Honesty is doing the job without being influenced by financial self-interest. It is always possible for a subordinate to have a conflict of interest about the way that he does his job because of his outside activities.

Many federal appointees have been questioned about possible conflict of interest in their serving in important foreign policy positions because of the nature of their personal clients. In many cases—perhaps this one—the conflict is more perceptual than real; but there have been cases where a subordinate's financial self-interest was served at the expense of his job. The recent IRS and HUD scandals fully illustrate this. This kind of conduct is being dishonest at the expense of our boss. No loyal subordinate would become so involved.

• Honesty is putting aside our own emotional bias. Honesty is about doing what is best for the job versus serving our own personal emotional bias—or letting our emotional bias impact our judgments.

We can, almost unwittingly, serve our personal emotional needs in the ways that we do our jobs. In reality, this is being dishonest. When we behave in harsh and arbitrary ways toward the important others whom our job serves, we are not serving our boss's best interest. When we make decisions based only upon our own personal perceptions and emotions, we may not be serving our boss's best interests.

Emotional honesty is insuring that our decisions and behavior are consistent with what it is that our bosses want the job to be and to mean: we enhance his philosophy and do not subvert it by what we do.

A good example of policy-subversion is what sometimes occurs in the effort to afford equal opportunity to minorities. Policies have frequently been subverted because of the prejudices and emotional bias of a subordinate. Actions have not fulfilled policies. This is dishonest behavior.

I was once part of an organization that was responsible for providing the supplies for a mountain-surveying-and-mapping operation. The people doing the field work needed winter garb, film, chains, and special equipment of all kinds. The person in charge of issuance hated our boss. As a consequence, he made it hard for anyone of any rank to easily and quickly get anything they needed in order to do their job. He required requisitions, no matter how trivial, with multiple approvals. He required written justification of the need, no matter how inconsequential. He required several days lead-time for a requisition. He required that the used item be returned before a replacement was issued (the back of a tablet or the stub of a pencil). This is called "exercising negative power." Of course he justified it all under the guise of "protecting the boss." Sometimes when the heat came, he would give in; but he always did so with bad grace and complained about the problem he would have with our boss because he was bending the boss' rules!

As a result, this man was thoroughly disliked and our boss was hated. Our boss was thought of as the S.O.B. of the camp. This man succeeded in making our boss look bad to everyone.

It all ended happily one day when the inevitable occurred —this man was ill for an extended period and our boss took over his job. The boss was horrified with the cumbersome red tape that he found, and he was heartsick about the terrible reputation that he had acquired at the hands of this vengeful subordinate. He quickly corrected both by throwing out the unreasonable procedures and by making the customer's needs our highest priority for action.

• Honesty is not served when we use our jobs to get even with our boss—to serve our own vindictive ends. When I was Deputy Under Secretary of State. I had a subordinate who, it turned out, hated me. His hate stemmed from his philosophic differences with my policies. The way he took to vent his hatred was to punish me by the way he elected to do his job —which caused me to be relentlessly questioned by a powerful committee of the U.S. Senate.

"The Ship of State is the only vessel with which I am familiar that leaks mainly at the top," said Secretary of State Dean Rusk one time when we were directed by the President's office to "shut off those damned leaks to the press!" (Often the source of the leaks was at or near the top.)

Leaks are an irritant, and every President sooner or later becomes so aggravated with people giving unauthorized tidbits to the press that he reacts quite violently. This is a predictable pattern. "Leaks must stop! Leakers must be found and punished!" Aggressive steps are often taken by the President and his people to stop the leaks and to find the leakers—lie-detector tests, oaths, rigid rules of conduct, and other harsh but quite futile remedies. The leaks continue!

It was obvious that there was a serious security leak in the State Department. The most sensitive and secret information in any office is the content of people's personnel files, including the information uncovered about them in the course of a thorough security investigation. Every indiscretion, every transgression, every error of judgement, every embarrassing incident, and every private relationship gets into those files. And, of course, those files are also kept secret from the individuals concerned—even they don't know what is contained in them.

Information from those files was getting to the Congress and to the press.

Recognizing the devastating impact that dissemination of this information could have on the lives of people, Congress passed a law which prohibited any person responsible for personnel files from revealing to any unauthorized person the contents of those files. Specifically, the membership of the U.S. Congress was named as not being authorized to receive such information unless the head of an agency made a personal determination to release it.

The early days of the Kennedy Administration came close upon the heels of the McCarthy era. During that sad period in the Eisenhower Administration, the U.S. Foreign Service and the State Department were the most scarred of all agencies from the inquisitorial impact of those dreadful days. A McCarthy henchman was appointed to supervise the Security Division of the State Department, and under his authority a witch-hunt ensued that ruined the careers and broke the lives of dozens of reputable people in the Department. Few if any Communists were found, but the fear of McCarthy hung over the whole State Department like a pall. And the chief problems were legitimate life problems: "If I predict that something is likely to happen in a country as the result of X or Y, and then for any number of reasons if it does or does not happen, will I be found guilty for what I reported? Or, will I be punished if I am right?" For example, Foreign Service officers had reported for years about the weakness of Chiang Kai-shek in China and the danger of the Communists. When the Communists did take over, somehow those officers who had made these predictions were suspect! "Did they have a too-close association with the Communists? Were they in on the plot? They will bear watching!"

Another case centered around the officers who were in Cuba when Baptista was overthrown by Castro. "Were they too friendly to Castro? Did they somehow help Castro come to power?"

No one was safe from the suspicion and the inquisition.

When the Kennedy Administration came into power, many of those hard-line McCarthy security people were still in place in the State Department. Among a number of responsibilities, I was in charge of security. It was my job to stop the witch-hunting, to restore credibility to the basic reporting function of State Department officers abroad, and to ensure above all else that no information from anyone's personnel file was being delivered to anybody without the personal authorization of Dean Rusk, Secretary of State.

Yet we had a leak!

Day after day I would be called up before the Internal Security

Subcommittee of the Senate to be grilled as to why certain people were given security clearances, how investigations were conducted, and to defend specific actions. It was obvious to us all from the questions that the Senators had access to the raw data from our files. Someone in our own department was leaking.

The motivation for leaking can be varied: sometimes a person leaks information in order to feel important and to gain a sense of self; sometimes the motivation is to get his point of view expressed to the public when it seems that a contrary decision is about to be made. At other times, people leak information in order to punish their bosses or others in power with whom they are angry. And it is quite common for people to leak information for money (this is sometimes called "spying"!).

A leak to the Senate was not in itself so bad, but the concern we felt was twofold: first, obviously we had someone on our staff who felt so disgruntled with us and our policies that he took this opportunity to punish us; and second, if that person decided to punish us even more severely, he might elect to leak the same material to the press! In both cases, the leaker would be acting illegally, but apparently that was not a deterrent in this case.

We elected to call upon the FBI to investigate the situation. Some weeks later we received their report, and they had found our leaker. He was a McCarthy holdover. He was angry at the new procedures and new policies that we had instituted, and the new people (including me) with whom he had to deal. He justified his taking the law into his own hands by saying, "I feel it is my higher duty to my country to reveal the terrible security risks that this new Administration is bringing into the government. My superior, Mr. Crockett, has been the one who negated almost all of my decisions. He is a dangerous man! I am willing to sacrifice my career to bring this practice to a halt and to force Mr. Crockett's departure!"

Of course the committee denied the charges even though the FBI had fingered the committee as the recipient of the information. But the leaks stopped and their inquisitorial attitude toward us soon softened. As a result, we developed a more collaborative and less adversarial relationship with the committee. This served everyone well—the Congress, the State Department, and the public.

The leaker? He was fired by the State Department, but he appealed our action and the appeal dragged on for many years. Finally the State Department's action was sustained and the leaker was discharged.

• Honesty in giving the boss information.

There are two kinds of information that we subordinates are obligated to give to our bosses. These are

— feedback about what our clients and important others are telling us, bad as well as good, about our service and our product. The boss may not like to hear it, may disregard it, may get mad at our telling him; but still we must!

Not long ago I left a restaurant because of the poor service that we were getting. The manager was not there and I urged the person in charge to tell the manager of our dissatisfaction. Whether he did or not is questionable, but if he were really honest with his boss he would have done so!

— feedback to our boss about the things that he is doing or not doing that are both effective and ineffective. This has some potential risk for the subordinate because some bosses may be defensive about hearing negative things about themselves.

I once had a boss who was literally desk-bound. He never got out to visit "the troops." This behavior made him appear mysterious, removed and disinterested. Rather than confront him with his behavior, I arranged for a series of onsite visits. He met people, listened to their feedback about their work, and gradually came to look forward to these occasions.

But it doesn't always work. During the Vietnam conflict I recall suggesting to Dean Rusk that we stop using euphemisms for our military involvement there and start calling it war—in fact have Congress declare war. The result—I got a lecture on the fact that there had been no declared wars since World War II and the U.S. was not about to be the first to break that record!

Another time that it didn't work was when I was with IBM. I worked for Gilbert Jones, the president of IBM World Trade (the international division). He was a very nice boss—kind, tough, considerate, demanding, and very wise in the ways of IBM. He made my job easy by making me, a rank outsider, feel right at home. I was an "IBM-er"!

I went with him to the World Trade Sales Convention in Paris. I recall that the head of IBM operations in one country expressed serious concern that the IBM machines, used by one of the big banking chains of his country, were not fully meeting their needs. The machines were too "American" and did not fit the unique European ways of doing business. He urged IBM to "fix" the problems as soon as possible, or we would risk losing the account. Sure enough, some time later that banking chain cancelled their IBM contract and went with our European competitor. The IBM director was immediately transferred to a lower position, signaling his disgrace.

I remonstrated with Mr. Jones about the unfairness of the IBM action. He said, "Bill, I appreciate your concern and even agree that what we have done to Mr. X is not entirely fair. But you must learn that IBM was not built by accepting excuses of subordinates for their failure. The same thing happened to me some years ago. It is not a permanent disgrace. What it does do is make a strong signal to all of IBM that our hallmark is excellence and no excuses for failure will be accepted."

• Honesty is observing the letter and the spirit of the law.

One might reasonably ask, "Isn't there anything a subordinate should not do in order to please his boss?" Of course, the answer is "Yes, there is one line of conduct that no subordinate should ever give a thought to doing, and that is anything that is illegal!"

Illegal conduct can only end in tragedy for all concerned and most especially for the naive subordinate who, out of misplaced loyalty or commitment to a cause, lets himself be used in this way by a superior. When the chips are down, the historical record will show two things: the superior may often hide and let the subordinate take the punishment; and even if the superior steps forth, this does not take the subordinate off the hook for having acted illegally. The simplistic but powerful answer is "never step across the line of legality!"

Our most recent and tragic example of this is Colonel North and the Iran/Contra affair. While the Colonel's criminal sentence was eventually overturned and while many people agreed with his actions, still others thought that he had ruined both his career and his life by stepping over the legal line. The same is true in the financial world of junk bonds and inside trading. The moral: keep it legal!

The problem of ethical and moral conduct is quite a different matter, however. Ethics and morals are more soft-data oriented and mostly what the person involved has defined them to be. Therefore, whether or not a person crosses his own ethical line to accommodate a demanding boss is pretty much up to the person himself. He must decide, and in deciding, he must be willing to take the consequences.

CONCLUSION:

Honesty is an absolute quality—like pregnancy there is no such thing as being a little bit honest. We are honest in the things that I have mentioned above or we are dishonest.

It is my personal firm belief that honesty not only is the best policy for us to follow in all aspects of our work and our relationships, both up and down, but it is the only policy.

So—the leader-manager must, in his upward relationships, become known—well known—for the fact that he is honest. Not only is his word his bond, but his work policies and his work objectives are also honest.

This is the road to serene nights of sleep and fulfilling days of work. It is one of the most important keystone qualities of a leader-manager. It also is another seed of trust.

Chapter Four

Performance—The Third Keystone Quality

Our Hallmark Is Our Excellence

"An acre of performance is worth the whole world of promise."

A job comes into being when a person who is responsible for getting something done finds that he needs help. He then decides what the help is that he needs—he defines the job. After going through whatever bureaucratic processes are required to bring it into being, the job exists and awaits somebody to fill it. That "somebody" will be a person who fits our definition of a subordinate.

It is we, the subordinates, who actually make the job; for a job is nothing until a person sits down at the desk to do it. There may be a desk and chair, telephone, some books and maybe a job description, but the job has no reality without us, because there is no activity. When we enter on the scene, we immediately give the job reality and substance. The job takes on the force and character that we give to it; it grows in power and influence as we cause it to do so; it is seen by others as being useful, helpful and important according to the way that we do the job. We make the job by our performance in it!

The job also makes us. The job becomes us and we become the job. In the eyes of others, we become competent or incompetent, concerned or careless, helpful or uncaring, friendly or aloof, by the ways that we treat people in the performance of our job. The excellence that we achieve in the performance of the various tasks of the job will make our reputation with all who meet us or use our services. Most important, we will impress our boss, his colleagues and his clients with our excellence and our skill; and, of course, these clients and colleagues may tell our boss how pleased they are with the service they receive from us.

This being the case, the job deserves our best. Excellence must be our hallmark, and professionalism must be our goal. We must forget such commonly-heard phrases as "it's about right," "that probably will be okay," and so on. The hard-data aspects of our job must be done "exactly right" and "absolutely okay."

Our job may be the most important activity that is taking place in our lives. This is true because it is both present-and-future directed. The way that we do our job is the key to our present success and happiness in our work. Doing it not just well but with excellence will garner us praise and recognition. By the way that we do our here-and-now job is also the key to our future. People get promoted on the basis of their performance. When we do our job well, we gain the attention and recognition of our boss, and this forms the basis for his decision to give us a promotion. The speed with which we climb up that long, long ladder of success is keyed to the quality of our job performance.

As we have already discussed, a subordinate is judged to be dynamic by his boss only if he fulfills the expectations of his boss—gets the job done that the boss wants done. It is the subordinate's responsibility to initiate discussions with the boss to surface the expectations of the boss. The wise subordinate will find out from his boss the job's accountabilities, its goals, its content, its priorities, its methodology, its standards, the reports required, etc. Boss/subordinate discussions around the context and meanings of the subordinate's job can be a dynamic and exhilarating experience for a subordinate. If a subordinate will take the pains to be objective in documenting his case, and if he will present the facts as being his genuine concern for the boss, the subsequent discussion will be free from emotion, tension and acrimony. It will be a win/win for both the boss and the subordinate.

But the quality of our performance is measured by our boss on a very large scale of important activities. This means that we must be aware of several important pieces of data.

We must learn to know our boss as a person—we must be aware of his wants, his needs, his hot buttons, his values, and especially his dislikes; for only if we know him well can we serve him well.

Some of this learning will come from carefully listening to the boss and what he says about the situation at hand. Once when I was late for an official social function, my boss said loudly, "Bill is late for our meeting because he thinks more of those outside clients of his than he does of us!" Was he really saying that he didn't like me doing so much outside work? It was a remark that one could easily let slide, but it did have a message that the "listening" subordinate should heed.

Some of this learning will come from hard experience— from the things that we have done or not done which obviously irritate the boss. When I traveled abroad with Vice President Johnson as his arrangement officer, I learned on the first trip that LBJ didn't like showers so low that the flow hit him in the stomach; that he didn't like to stay at the host country's official guest house (too isolated—he wanted to be close to his staff); that he didn't like screaming motorcycle escorts, and so on. The wise subordinate will be surprised the first time. There need be no second time, for from then on he will do things as his boss likes them done.

Some of this learning will come from our paying attention to the experience of others and what they have to say about their dealings with our boss. The dynamic subordinate needn't learn all of life's lessons the hard way—by his own experience. So he will talk to people who are also close to the boss about their own observations and experiences, and thus pick up from them some valuable do's and don'ts.

It is but common sense for us to observe and learn what causes our boss to be angry, stressed, and difficult, so that we can act accordingly. It is not a matter of our catering to him—it is a matter of our helping him to cope with the difficulties of his own job. We must learn to know him and to understand him if we are to be effective subordinates! Once we know our boss, we can then come closer to meeting his deep-felt needs.

The concept of needs being a force in human beings that generates strong emotions, which, in turn, initiates behavior designed to fulfill those unmet needs was enunciated by the great psychologist, Abraham Maslow. It was he who made us aware of the potential behavioral consequences of four strongly-felt and unmet needs—security, inclusion, power and ego. But the problem that needs pose for people who are linked together in a relationship of almost any kind is that each of them has their own set of needs. Bosses and subordinates, husbands and wives, parents and children, etc., all have their own needs. In many cases these individual need systems are in conflict with each other. This puts each person in competition with others in his attempt to get his own particular set of needs satisfied. Whenever this happens, there is likely to be conflict, anger and harsh behavioral consequences. When this happens between persons of unequal power—parents and children or bosses and subordinates—the strong usually come out "the winner" in some form or other. (The children get shut up and the subordinates get transferred or fired.)

It is a foolish subordinate who engages in such a contest with his boss, because he simply cannot win. The truly wise and dynamic subordinate is the one who has the ability to graciously, skillfully, and sincerely put the needs of his boss ahead of his own. If we can ungrudgingly help our boss to meet his needs for security, for inclusion, for potency, and for ego, we shall not only succeed, but we will succeed big.

How one person, the subordinate, holds his own needs in check while helping his boss to get the very same needs satisfied is neither easy nor well-defined. Some ways that I have seen this done follow:

— The primary need of our boss that we must address is his feeling of security. We must learn how to make our boss feel secure about our part of "his job"—the job he has entrusted to us. There are several ways of our doing this:

• We must make sure that we are indeed doing the things in our part of "his job" that he wants done and which he thinks are important. All too often bosses fail to make this clear with the result that the subordinate does what he likes to do or thinks is important. One way for us to insure that we are fulfilling our boss' security needs about the *whats* of our jobs is to list all of the things that we do each day for a week. Some of these will be what the boss has previously placed in the job, and some will be our own loadings. We should then take the list to the boss and ask him to go over it with us. In this way, we will not only find out what it is we are doing that he values, but we will also find out what he is neutral about, and perhaps more important, what it is that he absolutely doesn't want done! This can be an exciting and useful exercise, for we will succeed in our jobs only if we do the things that the boss values.

I participated in such an exercise between a group of subordinates and their boss. They were all very busy executives with heavy work loads and with briefcases full of homework. Through this process it was discovered that almost 40% of each person's work load was made up of things that the boss really didn't care about. Do them or not—the boss didn't value them. But more startling was to find that almost 10% of the subordinates' activities were things the boss *did not want done!*

• We must do the job that he wants done not just well! but with excellence! There is nothing more important to the security of a boss (as well as to the security of a subordinate) than the boss knowing that "his job" is being perfectly executed by a trusted subordinate—that he has nothing to worry about. Therefore, we must get our work (the work that our boss values) done
  — on time.
  — in the quantity desired.
  — in the quality desired.
  — free from careless errors.
  — with important clients left feeling positive about the ways they were treated.
  — with minimum waste of time and product.
  — with minimum costs.
  — with minimum disruption of work routines.
  — with associates left feeling positive and well-motivated.
  — with an eye to the future that detects downturns and changes.
  — with contingency plans for crises.
  — with an adequate feedback system.

This is the hard-data part of the job and the boss' basis for his feeling of security about us subordinates.

• We are accountable to our bosses.

Some bosses tell their subordinates little, and others tell them much—how, when, who, where, why, how much, how often, how deep, how wide, etc., but in the end, every subordinate must account to the boss for his stewardship of the assigned task. It is the boss' right to request this accounting and it is the subordinate's duty to give such an accounting. The boss must be told because he, also, is a subordinate to another boss who is looking for that same accountability. And so it works, forever upward!

A subordinate who, for whatever reason, elects not to account to the boss fully and honestly can't win. Withholding information, diverting data, telling half-truths, forgetting, lying—whatever the rationale—is the behavior of a no-win nonprofessional subordinate.

The dynamic subordinate will not only fully and cheerfully perform the function of accountability but will initiate it. The subordinate's challenge is to account to the boss fully and honestly and still retain a feeling of personal freedom and dignity.

In some institutions, this accountability is sometimes described as "accounting by exception." This means that the subordinate is only responsible for telling his boss about those activities that are not on target—things that are not going well. I would urge subordinates at all levels to be more forthcoming than this. I would advise them to tell bosses of the successes to celebrate, of the obstacles encountered and overcome, of the storm clouds ahead, etc. Don't make the boss guess and wonder!

I was once asked by the owner of an electrical supply company to do a seminar for his subordinates on communications. "My people don't tell me anything. I am always in the dark. When a crisis breaks, I have had no warning. My people obviously don't know how to communicate. Will you hold a seminar?" "I'll be glad to," I replied, "but I would first like to talk to your people to get some data from them." He agreed, so I did talk to several of his subordinates.

They told me that he was a miserable boss whose normal communication pattern was to yell, shout and curse! "Whatever we have to tell him ends up the same—he yells and curses. So why tell him anything? If the crisis doesn't happen, we avoid a scene. If it does happen, we get only one bawling-out!"

While I can understand their reasoning, I do not believe that this is either the honest way or the dynamic way for a subordinate to behave. Such behavior may avoid an unpleasant situation, but it serves to undermine the trust of the boss. It makes him suspicious, uneasy, and insecure with the subordinate, and in the end such behavior won't pay off for the subordinate. So face the music—tell him!

Most of us don't have to make formal reports on what we have done and accomplished in any given period. Unless we tell him to the contrary, the boss generally assumes that no news is good news—that the work is progressing satisfactorily and there are no big problems on the horizon. I don't think that is a good policy for a subordinate to follow. I think we subordinates should make it a practice to visit our boss periodically (at least twice a month), preferably once a week. The problems of knowing when, what, and how much to tell our bosses is a real one, but as my boss, Dean Rusk, once said, "your guts will tell you"!

These visits serve important purposes:
— They reassure the boss of our interest in his territory (our job).
— They help to get into the open tidbits of information that in themselves may not be of major importance, but if known by the boss may help him in his relationships elsewhere—with his peers or even his boss. For example, we must inform our boss when we have a problem on our desk that involves a friend of his or a person who is important to him for any reason. The risk we run if we don't inform our boss is that this important other will raise the issue with our boss over our heads. If the boss is thus caught unaware, he may make an off-the-cuff decision that cuts us out of the loop. The best course of action is for us to tell the boss about the problem and what we are doing about it. Then when that "important other" appeals to our boss, he can say, "Oh yes—Bill has told me about that and we'll be getting back to you soon with an answer." In this way our boss has the information to enable him to keep the ball in our court.
— They help make sure that our boss is aware of our progress on special assignments, important cases, etc.
— They help us to express our genuine appreciation of our job and the experience that it gives us.
— They help to "tickle out" feedback from our boss. Hopefully it is positive, but the negative is very important to us. Often bosses are reluctant to pass on negative feedback, feeling "well, I'll wait until something else happens, and then I'll tell him." One problem of the boss waiting to give us feedback is that by the time he does give it, he has so

much pent-up anger that it comes upon us like an avalanche! It is much better for us subordinates to get feedback as it occurs— so we should help our boss express his negatives.

— These mini-sessions serve to build trust and to make the boss feel included. If we can be open, sincere, direct, honest and not appear subservient, each of these meetings will build increments of trust that are at the very heart of our relationship with our boss.

• We must do the job in a way that makes the boss feel secure about us. Our behavior toward others—our management style—must be congruent with the ways our boss behaves in similar circumstances or with the style of management he has said he wants his subordinates to employ.

If the boss shouts, hollers and threatens, then it is at least in harmony with the boss' style if the subordinate does the same thing. But if the boss is calm and peace-loving, and the subordinate chooses to be violent in his reactions, there is no congruency with the boss, and the boss may well feel uneasy with such behavior.

I once had such a calm and peace-loving boss. Patience was his chief strength, and he believed that reasonable talk would erase all difference. One of my colleagues was a shouter and threatener. His main threat was, "I'll sue you for your last dime!" Every time he made this threat the boss would patiently remonstrate with him—"Don't make threats!" One fine day even the boss' patience was exhausted and the person was discharged. His behavior was incongruent with the behavior of his boss.

• Don't let the boss be surprised.

Finally, it is our job to insure that our boss isn't surprised by errors or issues, that he has the data he needs in order to cope with his own boss' questions and concerns about problems in our area of responsibility, and that we cover for him when he does "goof."

The White House staff does this for the President after most press briefings. The President makes what seems to be a rash statement, and the staff then cleans it up and releases what is was that the President really said or meant.

It is this kind of support that will help our boss feel that we are indeed there to help him when the chips are down. This is feeling secure!

— The second need of our boss that we must address is his need to belong. We must help to make our boss feel that he belongs—is a part of the job and of the people in the job, and that he is connected.. We must help him to feel easy about having access to his territory. We must not build fences around "our jobs"!

- Help the boss to own his territory.

All of us have a feeling of personal territory — my desk, my car, my coat, my home, my job, etc. They are mine and are important to me. They are my territory and no one had better encroach uninvited into my domain! All of us seem to possess and exercise this "territorial imperative," this feeling of personal ownership, of the things that are ours, including our jobs.

There is one area, however, where a person cannot exercise such dominion with impunity, and that is the job that the boss has delegated. It is still the boss' territory because the boss still has accountability upward regarding the success or failure of the job. The subordinate is the steward for the boss and is working to fulfill the job in the best way possible on behalf of the boss. The subordinate has been given only a temporary lease.

Some bosses, of course, will sometimes elect to respect the subordinate's area of responsibility and not intrude unasked into this domain. Other bosses make no bones about their right to tell the subordinate exactly how he wants the job done. Leaving out the psychological, motivational and productive consequences of such dominant boss behavior, there seems to be little question of the boss' right to do just that. The reason for this "right" rests upon the rule of accountability—"the person who is accountable has the right!" And since the subordinate's boss is accountable upward, it is his right to have full access to the subordinate's area of responsibility.

I once had a subordinate who acted as if he owned his job. He barely acknowledged me as being his boss. He withheld information from me. He would carefully answer my questions, but he never volunteered or expanded on the answers. He went around me to higher authority. He made decisions and took action without discussing matters with me. He resisted my every effort to pull him into my orbit. He justified his behavior by the fact that "he didn't want to bother me" and his belief that his job was to take the required initiatives. No amount of talk ever convinced him that he was not meeting my needs or that to do so was indeed any part of his responsibility.

He was a wretched subordinate and he made my life miserable. I was angry, frustrated and upset all the while that he was with me. I felt left out and impotent. Despite the fact that he really did the technical part of his job quite well, he was a failure when it came to developing a positive relationship with me. Finally I could put up with him no longer, and he was terminated. He never learned.

We must guard against being defensive about "our" job by claiming ownership. Since the usual feeling that we have about our jobs is that they really do belong to us, we often take a strong ownership position in our relationships with others, even our boss, i.e., "It is my job and you have no business meddling in my affairs." We sometimes resent having to even discuss what we are doing with our supervisors, feeling that they are being "nosey" when they ask questions, make suggestions, or come to visit.

An executive vice president whom I knew literally told his boss — "Stay out of my territory unless I invite you in. And don't talk to any of my people until you ask me first"! Many of us may feel this way, but hopefully we have better sense than to risk saying it. This kind of behavior is not being dynamic—it is being stupid! In the end, of course, we can't make this kind of an attitude stick, for most bosses just won't put up with such possessive attitudes nor abrasive denials. Most bosses want to wander around in their territory to see and be seen, and they have a right to know what's going on.

• Invite him in.

It is the wise subordinate who is not defensive around his job, but who invites his boss into his operation and shares with pleasure what has taken place with the job under his stewardship. So invite him in!

The dynamic subordinate will open wide the gates of his job to the boss. The wise subordinate will proudly show the boss the work area, explain the improvements, ask for help on problems, and seek the boss' ideas for change.

The subordinate who can share his area of responsibility with the boss with unlimited and uninhibited trust, in turn, makes the boss his advocate, thereby gaining additional trust and freedom. It's the win-way to go!

When we do invite our boss into "our territory," we may feel like we are running a risk. There may be things that the boss doesn't like—things he wants started, stopped, or changed. In fact, however, this is not risk, it is part of the process of clarifying the boss' expectations about what it is that he wants done in a job. So—when new wants and needs of the boss surface during a visit, we, the subordinates, are the gainers; for we have additional hard data concerning things that we can do that will please the boss. Furthermore, this is our chance to interest our boss in things that are needed or that we want to start—new projects that should be considered and new directions to be pursued. This is our chance to show off the people who have made special efforts to get the job done. In such situations, we are not showing off our job nor our territory, we are showing off our stewardship of the boss' territory.

The wise subordinate will invite his boss in on every possible occasion—celebrations of all kinds, birthday parties, award ceremonies, special days, etc. These provide the opportunity to show off the boss himself—to make him seen as a "good guy" in the eyes of our staff. It is our chance to help give him pride and stature and reality in the eyes of people. There is a management philosophy called "Managing by Walking Around," and we can help our boss by making it easy for him to "walk around" in his/our territory.

— Third, we must help the boss feel that he does indeed have power. I have had presidents of companies tell me, "I feel absolutely powerless in this job. I can't make anything happen!" One way to accomplish this is to obey him. When our boss gives us new priorities, new projects, new directions, and new work, we have no right to either refuse or to neglect doing what has been requested. Foot-dragging is a major irritant to most bosses. We have no choice but to obey the legal directions of our boss. To do otherwise is to court disaster—perhaps get fired. This is called insubordination, and no boss will long tolerate it. When our boss tells us that he wants something done, it is our opportunity to do it with good grace, with dispatch, and with a passion to make it come out right.

The dynamic subordinate does what his boss requires of him, even at some cost to himself!

John Kennedy, the young new President of the United States, was rocking gently in his famous rocking-chair talking to the veteran Democratic Congressman from Brooklyn who was sitting on the sofa opposite him. The President had called his old friend and political colleague, John Rooney, to his office to talk about the State visit to the African Republic of Senegal that had just been completed by the Vice President, Lyndon Johnson. John Rooney had been sent along as an official member of the U.S. delegation (to keep an eye on the Vice President?, I wondered).

The President's first question to Rooney seemed to confirm my suspicion. "John," the President said, "tell me about the visit. How did Lyndon conduct himself on this, his first official visit to a foreign country?"

The President had surfaced the universal question that all bosses wonder about all subordinates, i.e., "How well is my subordinate representing me and my interests?: is he truly representing me in doing the job or is he aggrandizing himself?; is he capable?; is he loyal? can he tolerate the ego-deprivation of being in second place? Is he competing with me for position and power? Do I need to watch my back? Can I really trust him?"

It was common knowledge in those days that Kennedy and Johnson had been bitter political rivals for the Presidency and that Kennedy had selected Johnson for his Vice President because of political expediency. Johnson was a sensitive and powerful person with a high ego-need. Could Johnson act as a master artist, subtly blending these three powerful ingredients—the boss (John Kennedy), the job (the Vice Presidency) and the subordinate (himself)—so that he would have a role for himself that would enable him to be dynamic in his new job? Could he indeed control his own ego-needs so that he could act as a loyal subordinate to the President?

As Congressman Rooney droned on about the wonderful job that Johnson had done for his boss, the President, my mind went back to the visit itself.

When we had arrived in Dakar, the capital of Senegal, the American Ambassador and his wife had briefed us on the health hazards of East Africa—the heat, the dirt, the lack of sanitation, the disease—and the risks we would take if we failed to heed their warnings. "Never, under any circumstances, shake hands with these people unless you are wearing gloves. Only then will you be safe from the diseases that they all carry on their hands. And when you go among them in their markets and other gathering-places, by all means remain in your car. And preferably keep the windows closed and the air conditioner running. Only then will you be safe from the sun, the heat, and the disease-laden dusts. These people are really dirty!"

This advice, coming as it did from the U.S. official representative to Senegal—our Ambassador—seemed like an act of blatant disloyalty. This advice flew in the face of our new President's policy for our diplomatic representatives abroad, i.e., "You are no longer representing just the government of the United States to the government of another country. You now represent the people of the United States to the people of another country! So get out among them. Show them the spirit of democracy that declares that all men are created equal!" And almost as a deliberate act of defiance and censure to the Ambassador, Johnson dramatically proclaimed Kennedy's message by his actions. He walked and walked and walked among those yelling, screaming, excited people! He touched them and they touched him; he shook hands without wearing gloves until the skin of his hand was red and sore. The people loved it. The press loved it. The United States was the hit of the celebration, for Johnson was the only visiting dignitary who had forsaken the official speeches and cocktail circuits to visit among the people! And he loved it—loved the crowds, loved the silent disapproval of the U.S. Ambassador, and loved the publicity that his actions gave the United States and its new President in the world press.

In those early days of the Kennedy Administration, those of us who went with the Vice President felt it our duty to trail along behind him in the heat, the dirt, and the stench of that excited crush of people. Congressman John Rooney of Brooklyn— fat, pudgy and citified— growled out of the corner of his mouth, "What does he think he is doing—running for President of Senegal?"!

When I finally gathered the courage to remonstrate with the V.P., citing the danger to his health, his response was classical: "This is a demonstration of democracy in action. It may be the only time that this country's leadership will ever walk among its people!"

The Senegal visit came to an end. The first visit of the Vice President to a foreign country was a success. He was pleased, as was his old friend, John Rooney. As a long-time Johnson supporter, Rooney was enormously proud of the way that Johnson had conducted himself in enunciating the policies of his boss, the President. He had been loyal and supportive in every detail! He had been able to control his own ego needs! He had taken the first step in making his subordinancy role dynamic and satisfying!

— Finally, our boss, like most of us, will have some ego needs of his own. And we, his subordinates, have many ways that we can help to fulfill those needs. Some of these are:

• Consult him!

Remembering that our jobs do belong to our boss, it is only reasonable and logical that we consult him whenever we are in doubt about any major question concerning our work. It is foolish to guess what our boss really values in our work, and it is of doubtful value to question others. But it is pure folly to do nothing, so the only alternative worth considering is that of consulting our boss. This consulting process not only gives us the answer to our immediate problem, it also helps to reinforce the boss' personal feeling of power and usefulness. It is evidence to him of our loyalty.

• Give him credit.

Bearing in mind that our job really belongs to our boss, we will be well advised if we make sure that our boss gets the credit for all noteworthy accomplishments that occur in our area of responsibility. We may have thought them up and we may have caused them to happen, but the wise subordinate will make sure that the boss has known about them all along and that when they bear fruit, he gets the credit! Of course, if the boss is any good at all, he will insist that the subordinate share the credit. But that is not the subordinate's either to initiate or suggest!

• Ask him for feedback.

The job that a person does is always emotionally loaded by the subordinate's perceived behavior of the boss, and most important, the subordinate's interpretation of the meaning of that behavior. Whatever the boss does or does not do in the course of a relationship day-after-day has implied (and sometimes overt) meaning for the subordinate about the boss' intentions and attitude. For example, the boss seems to withhold important data that the subordinate believes is needed by him in order to do a job properly; the boss doesn't invite him to meetings that he thinks are important; the boos looks at him in certain ways; the boss appears at unusual times; and on and on. In such cases. the subordinate supplies the reasons and the motives for the boss' behavior, and often those reasons and motives, in the mind of the subordinate, may portray the boss' dissatisfaction, or they may not mean anything. This can be the start of distrust, suspicion, ill will, disloyalty, and outright animosity. on the part of the subordinate. Over time, these emotions can build to the point of causing the relationship to end.

The sad thing about some boss/subordinate relationships is that often the subordinate's perception of the boss and the reality of the boss are entirely different. In such instances, subordinates have the responsibility to check out their perception of the boss' behavior and their inferences of the meaning of the behavior. The subordinate must discuss the matter with the boss.

The wise subordinate will carefully choose the time and place of the discussion. He will take the responsibility for the feelings that he has and the way he elects to express them. For example, a person won't start out by saying, "Boss, you do so-and-so, and that means that you feel so-and-so." Rather, the subordinate will state his own feelings—"I feel so-and-so." Usually the boss will ask why, and then the subordinate can describe his perceptions of the boss' behavior and the inferences he derived from those perceptions. This can be the be the beginning of a very fruitful, trust-building process that clears the air and becomes ongoing positive behavior that keeps the boss/subordinate relationship vital and unspoiled by the pollution of unfounded suspicion.

- Give him feedback.

The boss may play the same game of perceptions and implied meaning that the subordinate plays, but the boss may not have the guts to openly and directly confront the subordinate about the things he wonders about. The wise subordinate will make sure the boss understands his feelings, motives, and goals. Only the most constricted boss can fail to respond to the sincere searching of a subordinate for positive and helpful critique.

- Share your needs and your dreams.

Subordinates also have needs, and wise bosses will attempt to understand and fulfill those needs. But, for whatever reasons, some bosses won't do this or are unable to start the process. If we have such a boss, we must take the initiative.

A wise subordinate will not elect to feel hurt when he finds that the boss is not aware of his needs. He won't sulk in his corner. He won't try to find another job. Instead, he will let the boss know what it is that he wants. There is no way for another human being to know our needs unless and until we make them known. Oftentimes our needs do make sense to others, do fit in with the higher goals and objectives of the business, and can indeed be met. It's the responsibility of the dynamic subordinate to take the risk of making them known to his boss.

• Be considerate of the boss' important others.

There is one absolutely sure way for us subordinates to enhance the ego of our boss, to enhance us in the eyes of our boss, and to add many people to our win/win network. It is a simple way that requires little from us except courtesy and thoughtfulness. This magic I am referring to is our careful and caring handling of all the people who are important to our boss —his boss, his peers, his friends, his clients, our clients— all who come to us for service or for help. When we give evidence by the ways that we do our jobs and relate to these people that we really do care about them and want to please them and then actually meet their needs, we can be sure that our actions will be reported back to our boss! The law of reciprocal behavior in its most positive form will take over!

These people will tell him
— "That's a wonderful crew that you have."
— "You are fortunate to have such dedicated people working for you."
— "I have never received such excellent and courteous service."
— "The person that you have in charge really cares about his customers." And on and on.

These words help us, but most important of all, they greatly enhance our boss' ego and his feelings of pleasure and security about us.

CONCLUSION:
Bosses, like subordinates, are people, and people come in all shapes, sizes, capabilities and temperaments. Some may be very competent while others are incompetent. Some may be experienced,

and others inexperienced. Some may be reasonable, normal human beings, while others may behave like tyrants. Some may delegate, while others may insist upon inspecting the most minute details of the subordinates' work. There are no general formulas for what a boss at any level must be like. No matter who they are or what they are like, it is the subordinate's challenge not only to get the work done when and how his boss wants it done; but above all else, it is the subordinate's opportunity to do it with unbegrudging grace. It is only in this way that the subordinate's relationship with his boss will become positive and trusting.

One of life's givens is that most of us will live all of our lives as a subordinate no matter what level of authority we may reach in government or in business, so we need to learn how to handle that role effectively.

The single most important person in our work life is our boss. This is true for number of reasons.

First of all, there is our reputation. One of our most priceless possessions is the reputation that we gain for ourselves on the job. It is more important to us than all of the fancy titles, the big offices, the generous perks, and the high salaries that we have managed to secure —all put together. And our boss is the only person who can give us this valuable asset. What we are inside the walls of our own work-place determines our worth as professionals, and it is our boss' evaluation of us that makes our reputation. When we leave that work place to seek another job, it is our boss' high evaluation of our professional skills that is the most important thing that we take with us. So our boss shapes our professional reputation both inside and outside of our work place. The boss is indeed one of the most important persons in our work lives.

Second, there is our power. No matter how fancy our title or how imposing our office, we will have no real power until and unless it is given to us by our boss. The boss is the source of our power.

Finally, it is the quality of the daily relationship that a subordinate has with his boss that determines the climate of the work place and the subordinate's emotional health while on the job. It is our success in our subordinancy roles that gives us security in the present and affords us opportunity in the future; it is our success in our subordinancy role that gives us the power to do our own job dynamically and effectively. And this success results from our positive relationship with our boss.

In view of the importance that his upward relationship holds for the subordinate, the wise subordinate must conclude that the number-one priority in his work life is to convince his boss that he is indeed a trusted and effective steward. This trust must be solidly anchored to the reality of the subordinate's performance, not to his clever manipulations.

The vitality and worth of the boss/subordinate relationship is more important to the subordinate than it is to the boss, because it is the subordinate who has the most at stake! Therefore the subordinate must work hard to make and to keep the relationship positive. The wise subordinate will, as a matter of habit, see that he does more—gives more—than for which he is paid.

The message this should convey to those of us subordinates who are also managers is — we must of course do our leadership/ management jobs well, but by all means we must strive to do our upward relationship tasks perfectly. We must make ourselves so useful to our boss that he cannot get along with us.

This is the mark of professionalism.

Chapter Five

Personality

"Some people may be born with a pleasing personality, but everyone can learn to have one."

No matter how loyal a man—or honest—or how much work he can do, he will not advance far in business if he cannot work with others. This requires that he have a pleasing personality.

What is personality? Our personality is the sum of all that we are— our clothes, our facial expression, the tone of our voice, our carriage, our thoughts, our character, our aura, our attitudes—our whole being. It is the "us" that others find us to be.

Then what constitutes a pleasing personality? The pleasing personality is, of course, one that is agreeable to others. The way we shake hands, the expression in our eyes, our signals of interest in those whom we meet, our vitality, the friendly aura that emanates from us—these are some of the manifestations of our personality.

There are some things that we can learn to do that will enhance our personalty in the eyes of others. One of the most important of these is that we can move the center of focus from ourselves to someone else. This means our deliberately taking a keen and sincere interest in the other person's "game." We can do this most effectively by being a willing and active listener.

It was my duty/privilege to travel with Vice President Lyndon B. Johnson when he went abroad. I was the person responsible for developing his schedule and deciding with whom he would meet in each of the countries that he visited.

These kinds of official trips always made my State Department diplomatic colleagues nervous. They were frankly jealous of their own prerogatives of representing the U.S. Government in the countries and were fearful that Johnson would do something or say something that would either embarrass or obligate the U.S. As a consequence, he was heavily "chaperoned" by U.S. Embassy personnel wherever he went and with whomever he met. And of course he was always briefed on the U.S. position and almost told what to say. (To give him credit, he went along with these paternal arrangements.)

Before one of his trips, Dean Rusk called me into his office and gave me these instructions:

"Bill, I want you to see to it that the Vice President gets to see each head of state privately. I do not want him to be accompanied by the U.S. Ambassador or any State Department or other U.S. personnel. I want his visit to be personal. There is no person in the U.S. government today who can represent the U.S. interests and concerns better than the Vice President. He has a most unique ability to listen and to convey to the other person our deep interest in their welfare. He needs no chaperone. He is the most effective 'knee-to-knee' diplomat that I have ever known. So I look to you to make this happen."

LBJ did indeed take an interest in the other's "game" and created such a warm feeling of trust and confidence in the other that the conversation had an unusual quality of sincerity and depth. In so doing, he was serving his boss, the President, well.

Another characteristic of a pleasing personality is to tell the other person things about him that you genuinely admire. However, there is no place in this concept for cheap flattery, for it will always ring false.

As a result, it will repel, not attract. But if we take a genuine, heartfelt interest in others, we can usually find something about them or their work that we can admire.

I saw Vice President Johnson give a superb example of this kind of behavior on the occasion of the visit to the U.S. of the President of Pakistan.

One weekend, the President of Pakistan was invited to the LBJ ranch in Texas, and many of us regulars were asked to go along to help. We were waiting at Andrews Air Force Base for the President of Pakistan to arrive. While waiting, LBJ went to each couple and in a very sincere manner told each wife present how much he appreciated and needed the work of her husband. It was not a general comment about his work but was specific around the responsibilities that each must fulfill. You could almost see those women swell with pleasure and pride; and, in turn, each found a quality of LBJ that they could admire. When he wanted to, he could display a most pleasing personality.

At the heart of a pleasing personality is what might be called "character." Character, in this context, is the sincerity and honesty of purpose that shines through a person and all that he does. Character is composed of such things as a sincere interest in others and their welfare, a sense of caring about other people and the situations they face, an outward awareness of others and an empathy for their station and condition in life, an understanding of the needs of others with a genuine desire to help the person get those needs met, a self-awareness that helps us to do the right thing and say the helpful thing in our relationships with others, and the ability to tell the truth and to deliver the facts in a way that is not abrasive. It is courtesy under pressure; it is acceptance of defeat; it is the ability to relate and deal with power without being defensive, obsequious or fearful. It is the ability to graciously accept the requests and demands that power makes on us, and it is our ability to relate to others without being competitive.

These are some of the ways that one manifests a pleasing personality, and these are the ways that a subordinate at any level in an organization treats his boss.

There are some traits and habits of conduct that have no place in a pleasing personality. Some of the most obvious of these are bitterness, arrogance, jealousy, conceit, deprecating and badmouthing others, pessimism, self-aggrandizement, ostentation, pettiness, greediness, meanness, stridency, sarcasm, belligerence, timidity, cowardliness, and selfishness.

CONCLUSION:
Perhaps the key to acquiring a pleasing personality is to make ourselves agreeable to others. We must remove the chips from our shoulders and stop challenging people—especially bosses—to engage in useless arguments. We must be optimistic about life and enjoy the friendliness that we can cause to exist in all of our relationships. No person with a grievance can manifest a pleasing personality.

Even more important than our making ourselves likeable to others is our making a conscious effort not to cause another person unnecessary pain or hurt. In other words, we must really care.

For us to really care is the most selfless expression of concern that most of us will ever experience; but it is also the most powerful force in the world to create positive soft data (feelings) in other human beings. Therefore it is a worthy challenge for us all to confront and an important goal for us all to strive toward.

To achieve this kind of care takes the best that is in us, for we are required to reach high in our self-management process. We are obliged
— to curb our own actions, words, behavior, etc., that fulfill our own emotional imperatives. Don't say it!
— to exercise self-discipline. Don't do it!
— to keep from insisting on getting our own soft-data desires at the emotional expense of another so that we can say "It really doesn't matter!" and mean it.
— to make sure our soft-data conflicts result in win/win outcomes.
— to control our human propensity to read motives, attribute reasons and assume facts; to accept people and things at face value until and unless we get hard data to the contrary.
— to cease and desist reverting to childish feelings of resentment, anger, and resistance when the words and/or behavior of others trigger in us the playing of old parent/child tapes (childish habitual emotional behavior).
— to make our own invisibles visible.
— to help others to reveal their own invisibles.

And perhaps most important, we must take the initiative and

behave in ways that reveal to people
- — their importance to us.
- — our high esteem for them.
- — our appreciation of them.
- — our concern for them.
- — their special qualities of excellence.
- — our willingness to help them.
- — our trust of them.
- — our thoughts of them and their situation.

We can easily fool ourselves. We can make good excuses to ourselves about why we behave as we do (work too hard, etc.), but we can't really fool those important others who are the recipients of our behavior. What do we really care about? That is really what we want the billboards of our behavior to tell the world about us!

We have to abandon the "Law of Reciprocal Behavior" and not act in vindictive and hurtful ways; we have to forgive, understand, and spread positives, not negatives.

We are required to exercise patience and honesty, and be willing to sacrifice some of our own time and self-interest.

The carrier of our care for and about another is our behavior - the things that we do to and for the other, day in and day out. It is not a protestation of fancy words that conveys our care; it is putting genuine feelings of care into our everyday behavior. There is no intricate recipe - just behavior that says "I care!"

Bad news does not have to be delivered harshly.

Differences of viewpoint need not be angrily defended.

Honest criticism of another's conduct or effectiveness is not enhanced by brutal words and actions.

Directness is often a virtue, but not when used as a club to punish, ridicule or to hurt others.

A pleasant personality is a caring person and a caring person is one who treats others with genuine decency and respect. Honesty, loyalty, and performance are all important elements of success, but the agent that binds them together into a winning combination is a pleasing personality.

People can win for a time through ruthlessness, stealth, force, and shrewd strategies; but in the end it will be the person with a pleasing personality who will succeed. A pleasing personality is the mortar that holds the keystone qualities of loyalty, honesty, and performance in place.

The key to having a pleasing personality is our ability to subordinate "self" to the good of others. There is no place where this will have a bigger payoff than in our relationship with our boss.

Chapter Six

The Boss Owns the Job

"One of the greatest shortcomings of today's executive is his failure to do what he is supposed to do."

No matter how high we may rise in the bureaucratic world of government or in the competitive world of private enterprise, no job will ever belong to us! It will never be ours! We do not own our job. Our boss owns our job!

We often talk about "my job," and "my people." These are euphemisms expressing a relationship, not a fact. The fact is that all jobs belong to the boss. We don't belong to our boss, but the jobs that we fill do. It is the boss who is held accountable for the tasks that we, the subordinates, perform. It is the responsibility of the boss to see that these jobs are done well and are finished on time, and that the product is up to standard. He can delegate his authority, but the responsibility for what we do or fail to do is always his. The job in all of its ramifications belongs to the boss.

When we take a job, we are the steward — the person put in charge of something that is the basic responsibility of another; it may even by owned by another. While we occupy the job, it is our obligation to do the very best that we can to make the job prosper — to protect it and to keep it safely for its real owner, our boss. He, in the end, must account upward for what we have or have not done in our stewardship capacity. It is his responsibility.

One only has to experience a crisis in the job to have forcefully demonstrated the truth that the job belongs to the boss. I would define crisis as a circumstance that causes a job to become critical to a boss in one way or another. Such things as production failures, profit downturns, strikes, legal problems, etc., can cause a boss to have enough concern that he takes the job over from the subordinate. The Exxon oil spill or the poison found in Tylenol are good examples of crises that caused jobs to be pulled upward for action. We subordinates must prepare ourselves psychologically for this action that takes place when there is a crisis in our jobs.

I was Deputy Under Secretary of State when President Kennedy was assassinated. It didn't occur to me that his assassination would precipitate a crisis in my department, but it did.

When the assassination occurred, my boss, Secretary of State Dean Rusk, was half-way across the Pacific en route to a conference in Japan. Of course he cancelled the conference and returned to the United States.

Two offices that were affected by that tragic event, the Office of Security and the U.S. Visa Office, were under my jurisdiction. The first thing I knew, I and my managers in charge of Security and Visas were summoned to the office of George Ball, the Acting Secretary of State. He had taken over my job! My job had been sucked upward into the hands of my boss because of this crisis! I had forcefully demonstrated to me that "my job," despite its fancy title, was not mine! "My job" belonged to my boss!

A. He decides what!

In a survey, a group of top-level decision-makers and business people failed to agree on the exact acts of subordinancy that would insure the success of a subordinate. They did agree, however, on the point that a subordinate must know precisely what it is that his boss values. Doing a number of things well will not make a subordinate successful if the boss doesn't value or care about those things; no amount of effort in areas that the boss cares little about will make the subordinate succeed if he fails to perform well in the areas that the boss holds dear!

Some of the subordinate's misunderstanding about the job comes from ambiguity as to what the boss wants and expects of the job. The more ambiguity there is in a job, the greater the danger that the subordinate will not deliver what it is that the boss really expects. The failure of the boss to adequately define the job's goals and his expectations allows the subordinate to load the job with the things that the subordinate values, wants to do, likes to do, or thinks important to do. We can make ourselves very busy with these self-loadings and yet not be pleasing our boss!

When I was a young man, I was a teller in a small bank in Hastings, Nebraska. It was my first real job. I was eager, quick, and callow. There were two other tellers in the bank, a man and a woman, both older and more experienced that I. I was a good teller, I thought: I was friendly with people; I handled their business with dispatch; and I got them on their way quickly; so people liked to come to my window, and I waited on more than the other two tellers combined. In doing so, however, I postponed doing the things that were a part of each transaction (verifying the totals by adding the checks, sorting and putting away the cash, sorting the checks into proper categories, etc.). By closing time on busy days, my station was a colossal mess — checks unsorted, cash not taken care of, etc. It often took me hours after the other two tellers had balanced and gone home for me to get my work done. And, as one would expect, I hardly ever balanced my books to the penny. I would be over sometimes and short sometimes, but hardly ever could I balance my day's work. I discounted this fact. "Look at those long lines of satisfied customers that come to my window," I told myself. "My boss will see how many I wait on and hear of their satisfaction with my work, and I will surely be rewarded!"

One day the boss called me into his office and closed the door. "Here comes the raise and the commendation," I said to myself. You can imagine my shock and my hurt when he said instead, "Bill, I am very concerned about the way that you are doing your job. I get the impression that you are competing with the other two tellers to get the most customers. If this is your intention, you are indeed getting long lines of people at your station. But that is not what working at this bank is all about. The cardinal rule of banking is accuracy — balancing the books every night. That is my highest expectation of a teller. And I must say, as you well know, that you have been doing a miserable job on that score."

He could see my obvious shock, so after a few seconds he said, "Perhaps I share the blame for this situation because I did not make explicit to you my expectations of the job. But now you do know what it is that I value — must have — in a teller: accuracy in all transactions. Do you think that you know what you must do in the ways that you do your job in order to fulfill my expectations?"

"Oh yes," I said. "I will finish each person's transaction before I move on to the next one. This will do well for me , but what about the long line of waiting customers?"

"That's a good point, Bill," he said. "But your main concern, in fact your only concern, is to do your own job well. The long line of waiting customers is my responsibility, and I will have to figure out how to handle it when you start doing your job as it should be done. Okay?"

"Okay, sir — and it will sure make that job easier for me," I said.

"Good! We'll both be winners," he said.

I had made myself very busy by loading the job with work that I thought to be important but that the boss did not value! I was not rewarded!

CONCLUSION:
It is my experience as both a subordinate and a leader-manager that this concept of job ownership is one of the most difficult concepts for the leader-manager to accept. It seems to violate the most basic human security needs—this is mine!; but rich rewards of personal well-being and job success will flow to the leader-manager/subordinate who wholeheartedly embraces and fulfills this concept—"The boss owns the job!"

We saw this at work in the recent Gulf war. We saw General Schwarzkopf graciously acceding to the authority of President Bush to decide what, when, and where. General Schwarzkopf publicly displayed the best leader-manager/subordinate qualities, i.e., "Yes, boss—

you do own this job!"

This is one of the most important of all the subordinate's secrets.

B. He decides when!

"Wisdom is knowing what to do next."

The white telephone broke the concentrated silence of my thoughts. "Damn! Another call from that man. I wonder what it is that he wants now."

I spoke into the phone, "Yes, Mr. President?"

"Bill" — the familiar Texas drawl was soft and friendly, a sure sign of trouble! "Bill, there isn't much that the President of the United States can really do. But why can't he help a poor little man in Sicily have his son?"

I was caught off balance. My mind raced back across the days of conversations, meetings, and memos without producing a clue. What is he talking about, I wondered. What little man in Sicily? And what's that about giving him his son?

The President obviously grew impatient with my silence.

"Bill! Bill! Are you there? I'm referring to that letter you sent to the man in Sicily telling him that the President couldn't help him with medical assistance for his ailing son. Now, I want you to get this letter back, and when you read it, call me back and tell me how you plan to help that man. It's just a little thing for us to do, but it is life itself to that Italian man and his family! So tell me what you plan to do!"

"Yes, sir, Mr. President, I'll get back to you as soon as I get the copy of that letter. A messenger is already on his way to your office. Thank you for calling."

"Okay, Bill. And Bill, how are you getting along? Is there anything that I can do to help you? You know that I depend upon you and couldn't get along without you. So call me if you need me, and take care of yourself! Oh, yes, Bill, and another thing — when we do help that father in Sicily, I don't want to read about it in the morning papers. Do you hear me?"

"Yes, sir, Mr. President — we'll keep it out of the papers! And thank you for your personal interest, Mr. President. We'll keep you informed."

I was seething. "Damn! Here we are—beleaguered by the press and the public outcries about Vietnam, harassed by a hostile Chairman of the Foreign Affairs Committee, in trouble with our budgets and with a thousand-and-one important things to do, and the President wants me to drop everything to attend to a piddling thing like this!"

I had learned from tough experience that once the President focused on such a matter, there was no shaking him. I would be expected to attend to this one personally. The President's wants were not delegable tasks!

"Damn! Damn the luck that caused one of the clerks to select that particular letter to be sent to the White House for the President's night reading!" The State Department received and answered all correspondence addressed to the President from the citizens of foreign countries. From each day's batch of letters, we would send on to the President a half-dozen for his perusal as examples of typical overseas correspondence.

"Damn! Those clerks should have known better than to send such a letter! They should have known that such an appeal would pique his curiosity and challenge his ego to do something about it! I must speak to that correspondence unit about being more careful in selecting what to send to the White House.

A whole morning wasted! While I waited for the messenger, I let myself reflect on that call from the President of the United States.

"Here I am — Bill Crockett — a farm boy from Western Kansas, a career Foreign Service Officer without political connections, without money and without power, talking to the President and having him call me by my first name! What if no one had ever been interested in that person called "Bill"? Where would I be now?

"And then there is LBJ himself — a busy man, hounded on every hand by an unpopular war, taking time to rise above his own problems to want to help a fellow human being in a far-off land! This act of compassion would be without public knowledge and without political gain. A free act of human compassion! What a man! What a country! I will get the job done for him!"

My secretary interrupted my musings by telling me that the messenger was back with the letter. The letter was from a man in Sicily who was a member of the city government of a small rural town. He had a nine-year-old son with a deformed heart, a birth defect that seemed impossible to correct. But some doctor had told him of a new operation that a children's hospital in Boston was performing — an operation that created a miracle by giving such children new hope for life. His simple request was, "Will the President of the great United States find it in his heart to help me, a poor Italian civil servant, to have my son again by bringing the boy to America for the operation?"

"My God, what an appeal! And my own office had, in typical bureaucratic language, told him that the President could not be bothered with such requests! Damn!"

But, still, the questions came thick and fast:
— Was he a Communist?
— Was his son's condition really so critical?
— Could this be some kind of trap?
— Did we have the authority to do this?
— Where do I get the money?
— How does one go about getting an Italian child, without money, without papers, and without parents, into the United States, and without publicity at that?
— Would the Boston hospital cooperate?
— Could I get everyone to keep the secret?

• I put the Security people to work on the problem of getting the father checked out politically. Was he a Communist?

• I asked the U.S. military medical staff at the NATO base in Naples to get the boy's medical records and ascertain the accuracy of the diagnosis.

• I contacted the hospital in Boston and got their agreement to do the operation without charge and to keep the whole thing secret.

• I called my friend at the U.S. Immigration Service and got his clearance for the Italian boy to be entered into the U.S.A. at Boston without papers or documentation if accompanied by a U.S. Consul General.

• Cost? To hell with cost! We would absorb the cost into the Secretary's Special Fund for Emergencies in the Conduct of Foreign Affairs.

• I ordered the U.S. Consul General in Frankfort to commandeer a U.S. Air Force plane and to stand ready to make the flight to Sicily to pick up the child and to bring him to Boston.

Then I called the President and told him all that I had done and that now we would have to wait for the necessary wheels to grind.

"Good work, Bill! I knew all the time that you could do it! And I really hope that we can help that boy!"

"Thank you, Mr. President. I hope so too!"

I turned over the follow-up on the matter to a special assistant and got back to more important duties. What a mess!

In a few days I did get word from my people that the boy had arrived at the hospital and that there were no slip-ups in getting him into the country. He was in bad physical condition, and the doctors decided to delay the operation until they could build him up. I reported the situation to the President's staff and got back to my own duties. And I was busy!

The white telephone jangled again.

"Yes, Mr. President?"

"Bill, I'm calling to tell you how pleased I am that you got that little Italian boy in. I knew that you could do it. Did you have much trouble with our bureaucratic friends in getting his mama and papa into the country without the proper papers?"

I sat in stunned silence!

"My God, Mr. President, we didn't bring in his parents! That would be much too difficult an undertaking even for me!"

"Now, Bill, you really surprise me. In the first place, I know that you could do it if you really tried, and in the second place, I can't understand you, of all people, not making sure that that boy's parents are with him! How can a little nine-year-old boy who doesn't speak English, who is in a strange hospital without his parents, ever be expected to regain his strength? He's alone there with complete strangers to whom he can't even talk! It makes me feel bad and sad just to think about him! Don't you also feel a little bit sad?"

"Oh yes, Mr. President, I sure can understand how he might be a little bit lonely, but to bring his parents here is really asking too much!"

"Now Bill, I know that you are busy, but so am I. And I know that it may be difficult, but your President wants it done. Now you get those two people over here right away—do you hear?"

"Yes sir, Mr. President, I'll get it done right away!"

"And Bill, no newspaper gossip. Okay?"

"Yes sir, Mr. President!"

Damn!

But I did know how to do it—I did know what strings to pull and what people to push! And so I did! Mama and Papa were reunited with their son the very next day! And of course the President's office was told. (That white telephone on my desk was chiefly for incoming calls from the President for his convenience and not for my direct access to him.)

A few days passed in a flurry of activities — preparations for budget hearings, attending to urgent Congressional demands and seeing to a thousand-and-one other irons in all stages of overheating and overcooling! I was in a frenzy of activity! In the midst of it all, that white telephone rang again!

"I wonder what he wants now!"

The familiar, friendly Texas drawl came over the line.

"Bill, this is the President. How is our boy getting along? Have they operated yet?"

My special assistant slipped me a quick note updating me on the situation, and I was able to fill the President in on some of the details of the case and to report that the operation was still being delayed.

"Bill," he said, "you really did a fine job getting those parents in once you made up your mind to do it. That's one reason I like you and need you. You get things done!"

"Thank you, Mr. President."

"Bill, have you been up to talk to the doctors who will be doing the operation? Have you been up to see Mama and Papa?"

Again I was nonplussed!

"Oh no, Mr. President. They are doing just fine and I am up to my neck in our problems here — budgets, Congressional hearings, a bad press, and all kinds of troublesome things to deal with. I'm sure they are okay!

"Yes, Bill, I do know how busy you are, and much of what you are doing are things that I want done. But that stuff can wait, while human hearts and lives can't. So I want you to go up there tomorrow. Talk to the doctors. Talk to Mama and Papa. Make sure that they really understand the situation and do want to carry on with the plan to operate. I'll feel much better with you there. And, oh yes, Bill, come by my office in the morning and I'll give you an autographed picture of me to take to those folks. Will you do that?"

"Of course I'll do it, Mr. President, and I'm sure it will mean a great deal to the family for years and years to come. I'll go up tomorrow."

"Damn!"

"Thank you, Bill. I couldn't get along without you."

"Damn!"

So the next day I went to Boston to visit with Mama and Papa, to confer with the doctors, and to take the little unknown Italian boy an autographed picture of the President of the United States!

As I flew northward that morning, I was filled with resentment and anger about the President. "How stupid of him! How silly it is to take a full day of my time for an errand like this! Here we are — the President and I — battered by the press, fighting a hostile Foreign Relations Committee to bring about desperately-needed reforms, and he chooses this time to send me on this wild goose chase! Damn! How will I ever get caught up?"

But as I flew north that day, I decided that I must make the best of it. He is the boss and this is what he wants of me! I even found pleasure in the prospect of meeting Mama and Papa, of speaking with the doctors, and of delivering the President's picture to the little Italian boy! But, most important, I was also pleasing my boss!

CONCLUSION:
Yes, it is the right of the boss to decide when he wants something special done, even if it throws a lot of other activities off schedule. The bind for the dynamic subordinate is that he will feel obligated not to let the other pieces of the work suffer as a result. He will mange to get it all done anyway.

The real challenge for the subordinate is his acceptance of the boss' right to invade "his (the subordinate's) territory" and to rearrange his work schedule. Having accomplished that, the subordinate must refrain from becoming angry and emotional; he must recognize and accept both intellectually and emotionally that the job does indeed belong to the boss. Then he can, with equanimity, meet the changing needs of his boss. The boss decides when.

C. He decides how!

"Strive not with your superiors in argument, but grant their request graciously."

There is an old cliche which states that bosses do not give much attention to the "hows" of getting a job done so long as the desired results are achieved. This may well be the philosophy of many managers. If you work for such a manager, give thanks for your good fortune, because you will be as close to owning your own job as you will ever come!

One time I was Budget and Accounting Officer for the U.S. Department of State in Washington, DC. It was an important job, a responsible job, and one of some stature. It was my responsibility to present and justify the State Department's budgets to Congress. (One of the senators who was on the committee at that time was Lyndon Johnson.) Once we got our appropriations, it was my duty to account for the expenditures of those funds. We did our accounting the old-fashioned way — with pen and ink (oh no, not with quill pens!). After all, we were just then entering the computer era.

My boss, Lane Dwenell, was the Assistant Secretary of State for Administration, He was the former Governor of New Hampshire and was a free-enterprise, ex-CEO of a big northeastern corporation. He was what was called "a political appointee." He liked computers, He talked computers. He took me to computer demonstrations. He showed me other computer accounting operations. He urged me to start "my" accounting department on the road to computers. There was no doubt in my mind as to what he wanted me to do with "my" accounting department: get it onto computers!

In those days I really thought I owned that job — it was mine emotionally and intellectually. So, for weeks and months I did nothing. I never said "no," but I never made move number one to start what I knew he wanted done. But after all, it was my accounting department and I used passive resistance at its best/worst!

Then one day he called me into his office and closed the door. He was not angry, but he was serious. On the wall was a huge map of the world. The conversation went like this: He said, "Bill, for months now I have been trying to get you interested in learning more about computers so that you could get your accounting department started on a computer system. For some reason you have made no effort to accommodate my wishes. Now I have a proposition for you. You can find on the map Country "X" in Central Africa. They need a U.S. Ambassador there. The last one could only stick it out for about six months, but you might last longer given your great ability to resist! So my proposition is this: you can leave for Africa as Ambassador to Country "X." or you can get behind the computer program that I want for "my" accounting department. Do you need some time to think it over?"

My response was immediate: "Oh no, Mr. Secretary, I don't need any time to think it over. You'll find me the most ardent computer advocate in the whole U.S. Government. I am ready to start just as soon as I get back to my office! I'll get a task force appointed and at work before the week is out to develop a plan for your review and approval. I am your computer man, Mr. Secretary!"

He said, "Well, I'm delighted to hear your decision, Bill, and I have no doubt that you'll get the job done with your usual excellence and dispatch. But tell me, after all these months of foot-dragging and excuse-making, what made you change your mind so quickly?"

I said (with a twinkle), "No one ever explained the problem to me before, Mr. Secretary."

I had learned a hard but valuable lesson that day: Our job belongs to our boss. We are but stewards, and the job is his to do with as he pleases — even to changing the way that is is being done!

CONCLUSION:
Perhaps the most difficult intellectual concept any subordinate at any level will have to deal with is that his job does indeed belong to his boss, The higher one rises in the organization's hierarchy, the more difficult this concept becomes. At this writing the very popular and effective Chief of Police of Phoenix, Arizona, has resigned because he could/would not intellectually or emotionally accept that the City Manager was his boss and therefore had a right/duty to be informed of the Chief's whats, whens and hows. The Chief had forgotten the first secret of being a dynamic subordinate—the boss' right to be informed and to decide what and what not to delegate.

Chapter Seven

Trust

"Confident Expectation"

A. Building Trust
"Men cannot be forced to trust. Trust must be earned."

I have already mentioned in an earlier chapter that the only satisfactory relationship between a subordinate and his boss is a bond of absolute trust. Trust, of course, has two dimensions: the subordinate's trust in the boss and the boss' trust in the subordinate. Of the two, the one that is vital to the subordinate is the second—the boss' absolute trust in the subordinate.

Trust works like a bank account—there are both debits and credits. The subordinate doing all of the things that we have mentioned will indeed fill the trust account with credits; but the negative kinds of things that subordinates sometimes do can quickly deplete the account's assets.

Trust does not exist as a solid homogenous mass. For example, I may be trusted by my boss to do my job in his absence; yet I may not be trusted by him to make a risky business decision.

Trust is built in tiny increments of positive behavior around the things that have already been mentioned: obedience with grace, accounting with absolute honesty, unselfish stewardship, unlimited accessibility, and the courage to challenge and confront. It is built by day-to-day evidence that the subordinate puts the boss' interest first, does not upstage the boss, does not let the boss look bad, saves the boss from mistakes, rescues the boss from error, shows that he is truly happy in the job, and perhaps most important of all, gets the here-and-now job done on time, fully up to standard and meeting the expectations that the boss has for it. If a subordinate will do all of these things, one day his bank account will overflow with trust!

We have expectations for every situation that we encounter. These expectations arise mostly from our own past experiences, from the needs we hold about the situation and from what we want the situation to mean for us. And bosses hold expectations of subordinates. The fact that such expectations are not verbally expressed or overtly discussed should never be taken to mean that they are not held by the boss about the job and that they are not important to him. The person who makes such an erroneous assumption is not only naive, he is a bad gambler as well.

We subordinates must remember that when a person's expectations are not met by another, there is a feeling of disappointment. Once this disappointment is felt, a feeling of resentment and anger emerges. From anger there can flow distrust and a discrediting of the other. When expectations are not fulfilled, a powerful negative force in human affairs is set up. This negative force is one of the boss destroyers of trusting relationships.

It is always better, if and when the situation and the relationship permits, for both parties to share openly and agree upon their expectations.

Some specific ways that we can build the boss' trust in us follow.

• We must know how to do the job.

The value that the boss places upon a subordinate is in direct proportion to how well the subordinate enhances the effectiveness of the boss' domain, i.e., how well the job is done. The shortsighted subordinate conceives it to be the boss' responsibility to discover his deficiencies and therefore be the one to suggest training. The myopic subordinate thinks that his promotion and his success in the organization are his boss' responsibility. Of course bosses do have a share in these responsibilities, but all of these things are primarily the basic responsibility of the subordinate.

One unyielding requirement of us, if we are to be successful subordinates, is that we must have the skills necessary to do our jobs. It is our responsibility to look objectively at ourselves and our skills in relation to the skills that the job requires. If we do this and can see our own deficiencies, we can take on the task of securing the training and development we need. And if we are wise, we will also be looking at the skills that our boss' job requires so that we can be preparing ourselves for that day of opportunity. This aggressive self-examination is another way dynamic subordinates distinguish themselves from their more passive colleagues.

The dynamic subordinate doesn't wait to take on the responsibility for his own professional development. He doesn't own the territory, for his boss can fire him at will. The one thing the subordinate does own, however, and the one thing that no one can take away from him is his expertise—his professionalism. This is the most personal, most valuable, and most unique asset a person can possess! No one can hold a capable person back; his professionalism and talents will become known, will be needed, and will be requested, not only by his boss but by others.

When I returned to that bank in midwestern U.S.A. after World War II, the job that I was given to do was that of a real estate loan officer. I had not done this kind of work before I left for the military service, and of course my years of military duty had not given me experience in this field. So I didn't know what to do first. "There is the desk, there is the job, and there are the customers, so go to work" was the implied message from my boss. He did not ask if I had the skills to do the job, nor did I discuss it with him.

For a week I sat at that desk in sheer panic, almost immobilized by fear. What if a customer were to come in? What would I do? After a time, I realized that I must tell my boss of my ignorance and that I must have a plan in mind that would quickly bring me up to a skill level which would give me a chance to succeed.

So I talked to my boss. "Sir," I said, "I am most grateful to you and to the bank for taking me on after being away so long in the military service, and I am really flattered at being given this job. But the truth of the matter is that I don't really know how to do it. At this point I am really afraid of this job!"

The boss sat in contemplation for a few moments. I got the distinct impression that he was pleased that I had come to him and that, in fact, he had been testing me. Finally he said, "Bill, I am pleased that you have come to me with your problem. Do you have any ideas on how you might get the basic training and experience that would make you feel comfortable doing this job?"

I had thought about this. The management of this bank owned another bank in an adjoining town. I knew my counterpart there very well and trusted him, so I said, "Well, sir, if Mr. X in your bank at Y would do it, I would like to go over there for a month and work under him. In a month I can learn the basics of this job, such as what to look for and be aware of, and how to handle the special problems that come up. If I could be his apprentice for a month, I would gladly do so without pay or expense to either bank." He said, "I like your action-plan. I will talk to Mr. X at Y bank, and you can start there Monday morning. The bank will continue your regular salary and pick up your expenses during this period. Thanks for your honesty, and good luck while you are with Mr. X. He is a good man to train you."

It worked out very well for all of us. My relationship with my boss became a friendly, trusting one. My job was a real pleasure and challenge. It seemed that my boss' trust in me and respect for me started growing from the time of that interview.

The wise subordinate is the learning, developing, experience-seeking person who becomes independent because he is a professional! The wise subordinate never uses such maddening excuses to the boss as "That isn't my job," "I don't know how to do that," "I don't have time to do that," etc. He will seize upon every opportunity to learn something new and to have a new experience.

- We must do the job.

The dominant criterion used by our boss that determines his trust in us is how we do the job. The hallmark of professionalism is job skills and attitudes that produce perfection. Preferably, we will do the job not just well but perfectly! This means that we never let the boss down, never fail him, and never disappoint him.

Knowing what the job is and having the required skills will not get the job done if the person is not motivated to do it with commitment and enthusiasm. One of the most powerful drags on productivity in America is the lack of motivation of us subordinates.

When we are unmotivated, we are indifferent. Our self-esteem is as its lowest. We are slow-witted and sluggish. We can be so self-obsessed that we can't see the needs of people around us. We literally don't care—we are in the pits and it shows!

We can become demotivated by the climate that is created by the boss/subordinate relationship, by the pressures of the job itself, or by the pressures that come from outside the job. Wherever those pressures come from, when we elect to succumb to them, we let them make us the victim—we become the goat! We are on the way to losing all that we have worked for and have built.

If this frame of mind persists, we have several options:

1. We can take charge of our emotions and pull ourselves out of this pit of self-pity and despondency (easier said than done, of course).

2. We can seek professional counseling outside of the job environment. This is quite a costly way to go, but if it helps, the expense is worthwhile.

3. We can leave the job. This should be an act of last resort, but if we do not do something to help ourselves, the inevitable consequence is that sooner or later we'll be fired.

4. We can talk to our boss. Our boss probably will not be surprised when we tell him about our frame of mind. If he is any good at all, he will have seen how our work has slipped and will have been wondering how and when he should talk to us. He will also be speculating about the problems we may be having which have caused us to become so depressed.

When we talk to our boss there are two absolute, ironclad requirements for our discussion: we do not lay the cause of our depression on him or try to make our condition his fault by what he does or by the way the work is scheduled, by what others do or don't do, etc.; and we do not try to make it his responsibility to pull us out of this pit, to motivate us. We must assume full responsibility for the ways that we feel as well as for getting ourselves straightened out.

This discussion is vitally important for a number of reasons. First and foremost, it takes the mystery out of our behavior. The boss now knows what is going on with us and will actually be relieved that we have come to see him with our problem. Second, the talk itself will help to clear up some things for us that may be at the heart of our problem. The possibility exists that we have misread the realities that relate to us —the boss, the job, the situation, etc.—and we may have created our demotivation out of our own misperceptions. On the other hand, of course, the possibility exists that our analysis and our subsequent discussions with our boss only serve to confirm our worst fears and suspicions! In either case we will come out ahead because we have cleared away the ambiguity and now know where we stand. We can now do some objective action-planning for our future.

A supervisor once came to me to secure my advice concerning a subordinate who was failing in his job. It seems that he had become uninvolved and disinterested in his work. My first questions were, "Does he know how to do his job? Does he have the skills?" The answer was an unqualified "Yes!"

Then I said, "Since he is not succeeding in a job that he knows how to do, he must be having some problems with the way that you are managing him."

The supervisor said, "Yes, I'm sure that this is the root-cause of the problem. He cannot seem to accept the fact that he must include me in on some of his decisions. He cannot seem to understand that I am involved and accountable to my boss when he makes a policy change or a reorganization is contemplated. As a result, he takes the attitude that he will do it all—he won't get involved if I am involved. His attitude is 'all or nothing.'"

I replied, "I'm not sure how long it will take to make him understand intellectually and to accept emotionally the fact that he does not own his job. But if you are willing to take the time, we will set up a series of discussions where the three of us can talk through the problem. Perhaps he will see the light and we can get his productivity back to an acceptable level."

- We must be absolutely loyal.

This absolute loyalty means that we resist the temptation to whisper a weakness of the boss to anyone even though we know it will never be repeated. It means that we will not allow our silence at a strategic moment to cast a shadow of a doubt upon our boss. It means that we consistently and absolutely support him by never letting anyone suspect that we are dissatisfied or unhappy with his conduct.

I knew a man once who quite consistently undermined his boss by the snide remarks that he would make "in confidence." This kind of subordinate disloyalty inevitably gets back to the boss, and when it does, the boss' trust in the subordinate is destroyed.

- We must be absolutely honest.

It is quite easy for us to glibly say, "Why of course I am honest. I wouldn't take anything that didn't belong to me!" This is indeed one aspect of honesty; but there are four other dimensions in an honest relationship that we must be aware of. These were fully discussed in Chapter II.

- We must be able to handle difficult issues and people.

The boss may have total trust in the loyalty, honesty, and general work ability of a subordinate and still not feel comfortable about the subordinate's ability to handle a specific important issue. His lack of confidence may stem from the subordinate's lack of training or lack of experience handling such an issue. If such is the case, the wise subordinate will not be put down or fret about the situation. He will use it as data for his own future development.

At every U.S. Embassy abroad, there are American ambassadors who have been appointed by the President to represent U.S. interests in that country. They are highly-trusted individuals who are performing jobs critical to our national interest.

When I traveled with Vice President Johnson, Secretary Rusk

would often brief me on the heads of state that he wanted Johnson to see personally and privately without the U.S. Ambassador being present. He said, "There is no person in the U.S. Government that can do better knee-to-knee with a head of state on a difficult issue than Lyndon Johnson. So I look to you to make this happen." And so I did. The Vice President was trusted to handle difficult people and issues!

• We must be able to understand and fulfill our boss' needs.

There are three generalizations that we can make with certainty about bosses: all of them have needs; those needs will change from time to time as situations change; and if we are observant and sensitive, we can learn to know what the main needs of our boss are at any given time. Of course, the very best way for us to know for sure about his needs is for him to tell us, but life with bosses often involves more "guessing than knowing." By our interest and our behavior, we must make our boss sure that we do indeed care —

— that we care about his security needs. We make our reports on time, we meet our deadlines, etc., which will help him avoid uncertainty and worry.

— that we care about his belonging needs. We invite him to come to our parties, our celebrations, our meetings, our planning sessions, etc. He will feel less alienated because he has been included.

— that we care about his need for influence. We will seek his help with our important problems, include him in our important decision-sessions, and ask him to carry the ball occasionally with our important others. We will help him to feel more powerful.

— that we care about his view of himself — his own ego state.

• We must resist thinking that we are indispensable.

There are many jobs where it seems that the work never ends. We never quite finish one task when we are inundated by another, or maybe several. If we let ourselves, we might work sixty or seventy hours each week just to keep up. This does make us feel so needed and so important!

A frenetic work pace helps to soften the insecurity that we may feel about not owning our jobs. It helps to give us an illusion of importance, of being needed, of indispensability.

I knew a person once, a corporation's lawyer, who was never caught up with his work. His desk and all the chairs in his office were loaded down with folders, books, and papers of all description. He looked busy, and assuming his work was really important, he looked to be absolutely indispensable! What replacement ever could get to the bottom of such a mess?

One day his boss did replace him, taking the risk that all of those papers didn't cover up too many bombs. Sure enough, the company survived without him. He was not indispensable after all!

The job doesn't belong to us! The lesson for us is to cultivate, practice, and behave with a stewardship mentality, i.e., the job is ours to tend, to care for, to protect, to enhance, to develop and, if necessary, to hand back to its rightful owner, our boss! We are stewards. We do not own our job!

It has been my experience that one can find satisfaction and happiness in the subordinancy role if one deals with it honestly and unemotionally.

- We must guard against generating negative perceptions.

The way we are perceived by our boss, our peers, and our subordinates plays a powerful role in our success or failure.

"You know Bill Crockett, don't you?" "No—I don't think I do. Where does he work?" "He works on the third floor in accounting. He is tall and a little bald." "Oh yes, I know him. He's the guy that is always hanging out in the coffee bar." The fact that I don't always hang out in the coffee bar doesn't change the perception that I do. And if this is the same perception that my boss holds, then I'm in trouble!

Perceptions are the meanings that we assign to what we see others doing or saying when we don't have any hard data about the circumstance other than what we see or hear at that moment.

Perceptions are uniquely human. Even so, they are potentially dangerous for human relationships because they can be so wrong. It is from our perceptions that we form our impression of others. More often than not, our quickly-formed first impressions are wrong. But the fact that we are so often wrong doesn't deter us a whit—we go right ahead accepting our perceptions as facts. These perceptions and first impressions last forever. They are never completely dispelled, no matter how compelling the evidence to the contrary may be. They linger as little fingers of doubt, always shading the reality. Therefore the wise person, and most especially the success-seeking subordinate, will studiously refrain from indulging in unthinking acts and careless behaviors which might put him in a bad light with the boss, i.e., cause the boss to form bad impressions of him.

Since we subordinates are the ones who are responsible for the impressions we create, we are the ones to do the monitoring of our behavior.

There are some sloppy work habits that we can fall into over time. It is as if familiarity breeds contempt for some of the really basic and essential qualities of successful subordinancy. Some of the most obvious, blatant bad habits are
— being late for work.
— being late for appointments.
— taking excessively long lunch hours.
— being frequently absent without telling our boss our plans.
— not meeting important deadlines.
— not producing professional-quality staff work.
— not doing our jobs perfectly — meeting standards, quotas, and the expectations of the boss.
— adopting inappropriate or sloppy ways of dress.
— practicing incongruent behavior at meetings.
— not being prepared for important sessions.
— exhibiting peevish, touchy behavior.
— offering excuses for failures.
— wasting time by goofing off.

It is far easier for us to *maintain* positive impressions than it is for us to rebuild bad ones that we have somehow created. So, a word to wise: "Avoid doing anything that will create an unfavorable impression on your boss!" Each transgression of this advice causes a withdrawal from the "trust account" that we have on deposit with our boss.

• We must be careful how we use the boss' name.

When I was Deputy Under Secretary of State, I had a man working for me as my special assistant who was able and loyal. He got lots of things done, but I later learned that whatever he accomplished was at a high cost to me. The reason was that he continuously used my name to make our subordinates do what he wanted. "The boss wants this done." "The boss said for you to do so and so," etc. He became a real irritant to our subordinates and caused their alienation toward me because he used my name to make them do the things he wanted done. Our subordinates were afraid to tell him, "If Bill wants it done, tell him to see us," but that's the way they felt. They were angry at me for letting him do this. This caused me a great deal of trouble, long after he had gone.

Don't use your boss' name to get your work done!

• We must behave with discretion.

All of us subordinates expect and need the full support of our bosses when we have difficulties in getting our jobs done. And if we are worthy of that support, we most often get it. But we can conduct ourselves in ways that make it impossible for our bosses to support us; they may even have to repudiate us and perhaps fire us.

The 1988-89 Wall Street insider trading scandals are good examples of bosses being forced to repudiate the actions of subordinates and to disassociate themselves from the subordinates by discharging them. When we subordinates act illegally, act against policy, act in ways that hurt our organization, alienate important clients, etc., we risk being fired.

I once had a boss in the State Department who had been appointed by President Kennedy. His was a tough job, liaison with the House of Representatives and the Senate. He was an experienced bureaucrat and should have known better, but he locked horns with a most influential senator. This senator's support was critically needed by President Kennedy on several important legislative matters. Of course the inevitable happened—after a very acrimonious meeting between my boss and this senator, the senator called the President and said, "John, as long as Mr. X is your representative on the hill, you will get no support from me. I simply cannot work with that man. I'm not telling you what to do. But I am telling you what I will do." The President didn't promise the senator that he would do anything but, being a good politician, he knew a liability when he saw one. Not long thereafter, my boss was transferred to another less sensitive job.

Whatever the area, we cannot afford to become a public liability to our boss! He often will have no choice but to disassociate himself from us.

- We must fight our own battles.

In getting our jobs done, there may be times when we have legitimate differences with our peers and others. When the issue in contention is about the substance of the organization, the issue must eventually be brought to the attention of the boss.

Sometimes we subordinates quarrel over things that really don't matter insofar as the survival of the organization is concerned. The basis of many such quarrels usually is power, ego, territory, etc. Stripped of their bombast, these are disputes over petty, unimportant issues. The wise subordinate will not make his boss a party to such nonsense. It will annoy the boss and make the subordinate look childish. (This is apt to happen when we want our boss to fight with one of his peers because of our problem with another department!)

When I worked for Secretary of State Dean Rusk, he had one ironclad rule: "I will not become involved in any bureaucratic battles that any of my subordinates have with other people or departments over power, territory or status. Don't bring your problems to me!" As a result, I was pretty careful in choosing my fights — I only chose the ones that I could win!

CONCLUSION:
We subordinates will pay a very high price if we do things that cause our boss to lose his trust in us. We will lose our power, and we will lose our opportunity to be leaders-managers. Our challenge is to actively build a bank of unshakable trust.

Trust and how it occurs is hard to describe. It is created in the tiny meetings and exchanges that occur each day. It is the result of perceptions, of fact, of behavior, of attitude, and of the shared experiences of any two people.

It is the flowering of a relationship that is much more than friendship. It is a bonding of the relationship of two people where motives and intentions are never questioned and reasons are accepted at face value. It is a euphoric state to which all subordinates should aspire, for which all subordinates should strive, and where hopefully many subordinates will arrive!

In the final analysis, it is the absolute integrity of a subordinate that causes a boss to trust. Only when a boss trusts will subordinates at any level be able to do their own leadership-management job with enthusiasm and zeal. This, too, is a secret of the dynamic subordinate.

B. THE SOURCE OF POWER
"Our level of power in an organization rests upon the level of trust that we have created with our boss."

It is a fact of our managerial and leadership lives that we must have some degree of power in order to get our jobs done. It is also one of life's givens that, so long as we work for someone else, we will always be associated in a subordinate way with power. No matter what role of authority we may attain in government or in business, most of us will always be subordinate to some higher authority. Nevertheless, at whatever level we operate, we must have power in order to get our jobs done effectively.

Our boss is the source of our power. He can give us power and he can take it away. Which he does depends on how we handle our subordinancy roles. If our behavior causes our boss to mistrust us, we are likely to lose our power. If we inspire trust in our boss, we are apt to accumulate power.

In order for a person, at any level in the organization, to gain and keep his job and therefore his power, he must do two things with perfection, i.e., first, he must do those things in his job that his boss values; and second, he must conduct his relations with his boss in a way that he creates a high level of positive feelings of trust and satisfaction. When this happens, the person has job security and will be given power. Then and only then, will the person be safe in pursuing those special things that he wants to accomplish in the job! And the order in which things must be done is that he first builds trust and then he gets his job done. When the job is done in this order, the subordinate will be given power!

There was a story in the November 28, 1989 issue of the Wall Street Journal about the firing of the president of the Kellogg Company after only nine months in the position. He lost all of his power, the hard way, by being fired! Reason? He had, in short, failed to please his boss, William E. LaMonte, Chairman and CEO. When questioned, he gave "philosophical differences" as the reason for his departure.

When any subordinate at any level stubbornly and publicly differs with his boss on what the job is, how it is to be done, what it is to accomplish, and what goals and objectives should be pursued, he does so at his own peril! He will first lose the trust of his boss, and then he will lose his job and therefore his power! This was the case of the Kellogg president, and this is the fate of thousands of subordinates, at all levels, who fail to please their bosses.

The job that we have is not our source of power. Our boss is our source of power!

By being dynamic subordinates, we give ourselves the solid support with our bosses that we will need in order to exercise our power. By the exercise of our subordinancy, we have made our own leadership-managerial jobs more secure and more powerful!

Most jobs come with some increments of authority built into them. Even if it's only a matter of routine, that routine constitutes an element of power. The janitor, while mopping the floor, can put up signs saying, "KEEP OFF — WET FLOORS," which will serve to deny the most powerful persons access to the area. He is exercising the power that is built into his job. Of course this kind of power can be taken away at any time by a single casual statement of our boss: "In the future, I want you to first check with me before doing so-and-so."

There is no better example in American history of a subordinate's frustration over the curtailment of his power than the case of General Douglas MacArthur when he was in command of the United Nations Forces in Korea. His insistence on his right to invade North Korea against the wishes of his boss, the President of the United States, caused him to be fired. In the end, he had no power. Our boss is the source of our legitimate power.

There are four kinds of power. There is negative power, usurped power, legitimate power, and personal power.

• Negative Power

Negative power includes the power to deny people what they

want, the power to delay granting reasonable requests, the power to magnify the petty, the power to substitute bureaucracy for common sense, and the power to require absolute obedience in trivial matters. "Parental power," used either by parents or by a parent-like boss, is often negative power. This kind of power is used to curtail, to circumscribe, and to deny action. It stops things from happening.

For many of my more than 70 years, I have been subjected to this negative power. As a child, I was bossed and coached, pushed and pulled, and threatened and rewarded into becoming the person my parents thought I should be — the person that would be pleasing to them and worthwhile to society.

I escaped some of their direction when I became a student, only to find that I still had to live by someone else's rules, fulfill someone else's vision of what I might be and become.

Finally, I became a man, and as a man I thought that I had left behind that childish world of subservience. I found a job and at last had money of my own. This gave me, I foolishly thought, an economic independence that enabled me to be free of those old parental threats — "As long as you live in this house, you'll do things my way!" But alas, I found that I had only exchanged one form of domination for another: instead of a parent or teacher, I now had a boss to control and direct me. I had no power of my very own, even in my job! Since my territory was owned by my boss, he held the power. It was the boss who became my parent. The basic boss/subordinate relationship is much like that of parent/child.

It is the responsibility of parents to set limits, to enforce discipline, and to decide what will and won't be done at any given time. Parents reward and punish as the situation warrants. To a large extent, a boss assumes this same responsibility, so the primary feelings of a subordinate may be the feelings of a child: resentment, anger, alienation, and even a desire to get even. When this kind of negative power is used by a boss, it is very likely that his subordinates will use the same kind of power.

I recall a college food-service operation whose boss was a tyrant thoroughly disliked by all of his subordinates. He gave many orders, and woe be it to the person who disregarded one! One order was "Only I will open the dining room doors at mealtimes!" One day the inevitable happened—he was called to the president's office for a meeting that ran beyond mealtime. Students stood in front of the closed doors clamoring to be admitted while the employees laughed and chatted in full view. They did not open the doors, for "After all, you told us, boss, that only you would open!" This is sometimes called "malicious obedience" and is one form of negative power.

Most forms of bureaucracy are used in negative ways that deny people's needs "for the benefit of the system." When I see "no substitutions, please" on a menu, I know that negative power has taken over. The needs of the bureaucracy are being given precedence over the needs and wants of the customers!

The power-starved subordinate can use the negative-power potential of his job to gain a great deal of real power for himself. The power to deny is quite a safe kind of power to exercise, because it can often be supported by some policy or some obscure regulation. To deny is a much safer way to use power than to take action and cause things to happen!

The wielder of negative power is often richly rewarded by people who court him for his favors. "Get on the good side of him, butter him up, give him gifts, include him socially, etc., and you might get a 'yes' answer once in a while!" This is the power that our elected representatives often use, which makes the profession of lobbyists so lucrative! Wielding negative power does have its rewards for those subordinates who know how to use it so cleverly that their bosses don't get wise to what is really going on.

The motivating forces behind this kind of power are such emotions as fear, anger, greed, and vindictiveness—all of which hurt the boss in some way.

- Usurped Power

The second kind of power, illegitimate or usurped power, comes when a subordinate takes power from his superior. An example of this is when an army faction overthrows those in power, effecting a coup. This has occurred numerous times in recent years in Africa, Asia, and Central America. It also happens within organizations when a subordinate or group of subordinates usurp the power of the boss either by force or by deceit. The McFarland–Poindexter–North triumvirate is a good example of illegitimate power. When all goes well with such a group, when a coup is successful and popular, there may be no recriminations. But when things go awry as they did in the Contra/arms/hostage affair, then those involved are not only blamed but may face criminal charges as well. The boss is always suspected of complicity ("he must have been in on the deal") or weak neglect ("he should have been more on top of his job") or both! In the end, it is the boss who must accept the responsibility for whatever went wrong because the job belongs to the boss — and so does the accountability.

When a subordinate tries to usurp the power and authority of his superior, there generally can be only one result—disaster for the subordinate and embarrassment for the boss.

* Legitimate Power

The only way for the dedicated subordinate to go is to use legitimate power! It is only this positive kind of power that makes the most of our jobs and gains the trust of our superiors. This kind of power causes positive things to happen. It moves us to relate to and go beyond policies and regulations in order to make the job a vibrant, positive force, engendering innovation and change. This kind of power emanates from three sources:

First, it has its basic roots in us subordinates and our attitudes about ourselves. We dynamic subordinates would not dream of stooping to the sleazy exercise of negative power; that is a form of personal degradation which we wouldn't countenance. We are positive, action-oriented thinkers!

Second, it develops in proportion to the degree of trust that we have been able to instill in our boss. It is important for us subordinates to build an evergrowing, overflowing bank of trust with our boss, for it is only as trust is developed that the boss will have enough confidence in us to share some of his power with us. Without trust, there can be no power.

Third, legitimate positive power is deeply rooted in the degree of our own certainty about our job responsibilities. Power cannot safely flow out of ambiguity; it safely flows from our certainty about what we are expected to do. It is our duty as subordinates to get this made explicit!

When I was Deputy Under Secretary of State, I once asked my boss, Dean Rusk, about my job. "Mr. Secretary, what are some of the objectives that you have in mind for my job? What do I have the power to do on my own and what kinds of things do you want me to bring to you?" Since we were new associates, I did not think these to be unreasonable questions. After a minute's thought, he said, "Well, Bill, do everything that you need to do in order for you to live up to the horizons of the job. And so far as your second question is concerned, you don't need to check out anything with me unless your own guts tell you that you should do so. And if you ever go too far, I will pull you back!

This statement seemed to give me much freedom, quite enough to hang myself I thought, and it displayed a lot of trust in me. Seemingly it gave me a lot of power, but its ambiguity caused me to be uneasy.

We can graphically plot our job ambiguity and our legitimate power on a continuum, i.e.,

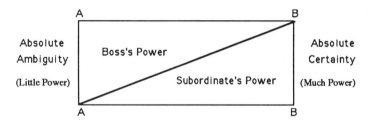

After my discussion with Secretary Rusk, my feeling of uncertainty was very close to line A above. My goal then was to try to determine more specifics about my job so that I would know my power base. To do this, I decided to make an outline of objectives, policies, and power statements for my own guidance as well as for establishing a basis for a relevant discussion with Dean Rusk about the specifics of my job— my power.

First I listed fifteen of the most important objectives that I thought I should achieve in the ensuing twelve months. Then I wrote a description of each of these fifteen objectives in end-result language. For example, one of my more important duties was to recommend to the Secretary of State and then to the President the names of people to serve as United States ambassadors. It was a built-in (although unstated) requirement that a certain number of these recommendations would be career Foreign Service officers, and some would be from the public domain. I also knew that President Kennedy wanted career people to serve as ambassadors at some of the major posts like London, Bonn, and Tokyo. I also knew that he wanted us to increase the number of ambassadors who represented minority groups, including women. I wrote:

"Objective #1: By X date to have in place 25 new ambassadors. The ambassadorial mix will be 60% career and 40% political appointees. The embassies at London, Rome, Moscow, Bonn, Tokyo, and Paris will be filled with career Foreign Service officers. Of the total ambassadors selected, no less than 15% will be minority."

I continued this process until I had a statement of end- result achievements for each of the 15 objectives.

To make sure that each of these objectives was shared by Secretary Rusk, I put an "Agreed____" and "Disagreed____" line on each so that he could indicate his approval or disapproval.

Next, for each of these fifteen objectives, I wrote out a policy statement that would be the basis for making subsequent decisions on issues and questions that would be certain to arise. These policy statements would not be ironclad rules but would serve as general guidelines for future decision- processes, i.e., who would do what and when, and how each increment of the task would be done.

Once in a meeting, I heard a subordinate say to his boss, "I am really confused as to what I can and cannot approve. For example, you trusted me to make the final decision on a $200,000 computer program. Then the other day you questioned me about a $15.00 bill. I am confused." The boss said, "It is all a matter of basic value and principle. I don't believe in spending $15 if it is indeed waste. This is the principle that must be applied in every case. What you need to do is to write a basic policy statement about spending money that will be understood by you and will satisfy me. Then all expenditures that fall within the stated guidelines—small and large—will not be questioned." Power flows with the flow of policy.

Next, for each of these fifteen objectives, I constructed a "power scale" that stated my power in getting each step accomplished and in what circumstances I should take the matter up with Secretary Rusk. The scale worked like this:

- Level 1
  I can make the decisions—no need to make special reports. (Note:

I listed the fifteen objectives with the specific activities of each to which Level 1 applied, and did the same for Levels 2, 3, and 4.)

- Level 2
  These activities hold some special interest for Secretary Rusk. I can make the decision, but I will tell him what I did when I do it.

- Level 3
  These activities hold some real political sensitivity for Secretary Rusk (or they are sensitive to others; or I don't have all of the experience I may need, etc.). I will discuss my ideas with Secretary Rusk before I move ahead.

- Level 4
  These activities are fraught with real risk and high-level controversy. Perhaps there is no clear-cut way to proceed. Before I do anything about these, I will ask my boss what he wants/advises me to do. (Of course I will come in with my own recommendations for him to consider.)

Once I had rated all of my duties and responsibilities on this scale, I showed the outline to Secretary Rusk. I explained to him why I had rated each as I did and asked him to share his perception of how the power should fall.

I made sure that I understood Secretary Rusk's final rating of each issue and why he elected that rating. In this way, I moved my level of certainty (and therefore my power base) quite a distance to the right on the continuum, greatly increasing both. The continuum now looked like this:

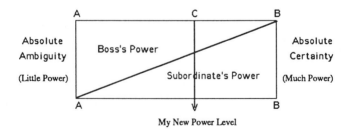

My New Power Level

When we had finished the session, Secretary Rusk said, "That was a good session, Bill. It got a lot of things out into the open so that we could decide how we can work together to make the most of our efforts. It seems to me that we have established the operating ground rules on about 80% of your job. I appreciate your taking the initiative in doing this because I frankly had not fully understood what the job of Deputy Under Secretary actually encompassed. Now I have a much better idea of what our objectives for the job are. So again thanks.

"And speaking of initiative, Bill, you have a great reputation as an innovator. We will consider the 20% of your job that we have left unspecified to be your own 'playpen,' your arena for innovation. Goodness knows, we need a lot of updating in all of our administrative areas, and I look to you to get this done!"

I was delighted with his remarks. "I was hoping you would say something like that, Mr. Secretary. The administrative apparatus of State needs a complete overhauling and, in some cases, remodeling. So we'll get at it right away! But how much and what do you want me to tell you about, Mr. Secretary?"

"Oh, Bill, your own guts will tell you what you should report to me. Just live up to the horizon of your job!" he said with a twinkle. "That is what that 20% freedom that you have is to be used for!"

This process is a good one to use because it does not in any way threaten the boss and forms an excellent basis for an objective discussion with him about our job—our authority and our power.

Perhaps the real basis for the Secretary's statement to me about the job was his own uncertainty. Perhaps he really didn't know exactly what it was that I was supposed to do, or all of the steps involved, or all of the people who would be involved. This is often the case. This exercise helps our bosses to become familiar with our responsibilities and our functions. It gives them an objective basis upon which they can evaluate our performance as subordinates.

The 20% area, the undefined part of our job, becomes the part of the job that we really can own, but we must always do the 80% of our jobs to the total satisfaction of our boss! Doing the 80% to perfection gains us the confidence of our boss and thus gives us the freedom to use the 20% for our own innovative purposes.

• Personal Power

Personal power, as a concept, has nothing to do with the kind of power that one obtains from the authority which flows from position, job or situation. It has nothing to do with the power that may be derived from money, education, status, or office. It has nothing to do with anything that is external to us. Personal power is a force within us which we can develop, which we can use for good (or evil), and which we can share with others. And strangely enough—the very act of sharing this power with others not only gives others power but also enhances and increases our own power!

There are two important facets of "personal power" that are distinct and separate, yet which are intertwined and interact together. There is, first, the power that we give to ourselves in the ways that we feel, behave, talk, and interact with others. The second is the power that we give to others in the ways that they feel, behave, talk, and interact with us and with others. It is interesting to note that the kind of power that we are talking about here has a positive "rub-off" impact upon all with whom we associate and interact. So, in a very real sense, we are literally giving power to others.

There are also two possible thrusts of personal power of which we should be aware, even though our interest is centered in the development of only one.

Our personal power can be overwhelmingly of the negative variety. When this is the case, we are mostly angry, bitter, sarcastic, uncertain, overbearing, mean, harsh, etc., with ourselves and in our relationships with others. This kind of power has a dreadful negative impact upon us, and, more important, upon all who must associate with us if we are such a person. Life becomes a constant emotional burden for everyone. Our power is indeed affecting others!

On the other hand, personal power can be overwhelmingly of the positive kind. This means that we are mostly happy, constant, straight, self-assured, turned on, forgiving, loving, kind, caring, etc., with ourselves and in our relationships with others. This kind of power has a wonderful uplifting, purifying impact upon all who are privileged to associate with us—if we are indeed such a person. And life then can become an ever-increasing source of positive power for everyone.

It goes without saying that it is this positive thrust that the personal power which we want to help you to build is directed toward.

CONCLUSION
The degree of power that we possess is directly proportionate to the

amount of trust that our superior has in us and the degree of certainty that we have been able to create about our jobs. It is our superior who is our source of power.

When a boss holds a high degree of trust for a subordinate, it tends to instill confidence in the subordinate and therefore makes him more effective in his leadership-management function. It is strange how it works. The subordinate does his job and creates strong feelings of trust in his boss. Because of this trust, the boss gives more security and power to the subordinate, which then enables the subordinate to do more for the boss. It is an endless positive process which has at its heart the certainty that exists between the boss and the subordinate as to what the subordinate's powers actually are.

This is the secret that every dynamic subordinate knows and practices.

C. THE SOURCE OF AUTONOMY
"The freedom to pursue one's own visions is the subordinate's ultimate goal."

"Captain Crockett," the General roared, "you have changed the format of this report!" He scratched a large red "X" across its face before he threw it back to me.

"Yes, sir," I replied. "I thought...."

"That's the trouble with today's Army. We have too many captains who are trying to think!"

I saluted and walked out, never to see him again! I had made up my mind—no more Generals for me!

I was a World War II reserve officer who had been recalled to active duty in the Korean War. My job was to make loans to industries that manufactured products needed in the war effort.

I spent the next several weeks trying to find a discrete way to escape this military service that put such a premium upon mindless conformity! And I found the loophole—I could be released from military service if another government agency would request me for "important overseas duty in the national interest." My friend in State wrote the letter of request, and this same General approved the request. He probably muttered while signing it, "Good riddance to another one of those thinking Captains!"

If anyone was to blame for this fiasco, it was I—I had not built a base of trust with that General that would give me the power to be innovative and to take initiative.

There are several things that we subordinates must do before we can exercise our creativity without fear of reprimand:

• We must make sure that we are fulfilling the needs of our boss in the regular course of our work. If his needs are not being met, we are in trouble no matter what!

• We must show by our behavior that we know that the job does not belong to us and that our time is not our own. This means, of course, that we are responsive to our boss.

• We must make it apparent that we understand what our boss expects of us and that we are totally dedicated to meeting those expectations. This means that we are doing what he values and that we are doing that well.

Doing these things will help to create a foundation of trust upon which the relationship between us and our boss rests, enabling him to feel secure enough about our motives to grant us the power to take initiatives and be innovative—to create new products, new services, and new procedures for getting the job done.

This new power may not be overtly mentioned by either the boss or the subordinate, but both know that it exists and both wonder, often with excitement, what it will produce!

In Tom Peters' book, "In Search of Excellence," this kind of innovation is called "skunk works," meaning that it falls outside regular work and administrative processes. It is going on because of the trust that the boss holds for the subordinate.

When I was Deputy Under Secretary of State, my chief was Dean Rusk. We had discussed and agreed upon the main responsibilities of my job, but, in the words of Rusk himself, there was "much more to be done out there. Fill the horizons of your responsibilities."

The "whats" and the "hows" of what he was referring to were so ambiguous that they couldn't be specified or quantified, making "out there" a fertile area in which to exercise innovation and initiative. And the Secretary had given me the power—the go-ahead—to do this.

Very often these initiatives have their beginnings in small informal settings where people gather to talk excitedly about the possibility of doing this or the feasibility of starting that. The opening paragraph of the book, "Programming Systems and Foreign Affairs Leadership" by Frederick Mosher and John Harr, describes one such setting.

"In the winter of 1962-63, a small group of individuals in the U.S. Department of State undertook the development and installation of a system to program the American foreign policy activities of all agencies in individual foreign countries. This later came to be known as the Comprehensive Country Programming System (CCPS), and still later with further modifications, as the Foreign Affairs Programming System (FAPS)."

This was the beginning of a massive "skunk works" program of innovation in the Department of State, whose purpose was to change the entire planning and budgeting system of the foreign affairs agencies of the United States Government. To further quote:

"The man who was to sponsor the State Department's programming effort, William J. Crockett, showed an early interest in the subject, accumulating thoughts and ideas during many years of service abroad as an administrative officer for AID and State. When he became Assistant Secretary of State for Administration early in 1961, he prepared a list of changes and improvements he regarded as needed in the Department of State, and prominent on this list was a new method of linking plans, programs and budgets."

As the following passage indicates, innovation, when it is seen to encroach upon the interests and territory of others, can become difficult for those in charge.

"Barrett (Special Assistant to Mr. Crockett), for example, did not hesitate to use Crockett's authority to cut through red tape and get what he wanted quickly, whether it involved buying equipment, demanding computer time, transferring an officer from another assignment to join his staff, or making a field trip when virtually no one else in the

Department could travel abroad because of a shortage of funds. He did so because he felt himself under orders from Crockett to proceed as quickly as possible, and because he believed that the end—the development of a programming system for all foreign affairs—justified almost any means. This view was not widely shared outside of Barrett's immediate staff. The administrative officials began building up a long agenda of real and imagined abuses. They were largely frustrated, however, since they, too, worked for Crockett who was supporting Barrett's group. But Crockett began to hear complaints, and for the CCPS staff almost every move involved a struggle with one or another of the administrative units in the Department."

By definition, innovative efforts are outside of the regular structure.of operations. They are often only vaguely known about and understood by top management, so these elders have limited loyalty and give only soft support to the effort. Thus, when the price seems to be getting too high for them in terms of other problems they face, they find it easy to terminate the innovation with no loss of face and no recriminations. "Another one that didn't work!"

This initiative came to nothing, as so many such efforts do. In this case the idea was valid, but the bureaucratic entrenchments, both in the State Department as well as other U.S. agencies, that the concept would breach were strong enough to kill the project. The power of the Secretary of State was not enough to overcome the strong opposition. But the point to be made is that this was possible because of the trust that Secretary Rusk held for his subordinate Deputy Under Secretary, Bill Crockett.

The fact that we have the power to be creative does not insure the success of our initiatives and attempts at innovation!

Innovations which are implemented outside of the direct vision of the chief and without his overt knowledge are to some extent risky. Their pursuit is part of the artistry of the dynamic subordinate whose self-confidence rests on three pillars of strength:

• The subordinate's knowledge that his boss trusts him absolutely. If the subordinate feels nervous about "what might the boss think/do," then that subordinate will not implement innovative ideas. A weak and "iffy" boss/subordinate climate of trust won't support the risk, so the subordinate will not take the risk.

• The subordinate's own feeling of self-esteem and security. This springs from many sources—from the boss and his degree of trust; from the subordinate's own level of professionalism; from the subordinate's support system, and from other intangibles. The innovative subordinate must be a self-assured person.

• The work itself must be such as to afford opportunities for designing innovative procedures, processes, services and products. In most organizations there is plenty of need and opportunity for innovation and initiative.

CONCLUSION

Innovation can only be built upon a base of mutual trust between the boss and the subordinate. The responsibility for creating this base is chiefly that of the subordinate. The subordinate who attempts innovation before such a base is created invites the anger and reprimand of his boss.

The dynamic subordinate will deliberately and aggressively build a trust account with his boss, will carefully delineate his area of power with his boss, and will perform the job in all of its ramifications as perfectly as he can so that he will be given the power and freedom to exercise his creative skills and innovative ideas.

In all too many cases, the leader-manager starts cleaning house, changing processes and planning new initiatives before he has created a solid base of trust with his boss. Leader-managers who fall into this kind of an activity trap before they develop trusting upward relationships may not last long in a job.

The old western adage, "Fill the bucket of your boss before you start filling your own," graphically describes the secrets of a wise and dynamic subordinate.

Chapter Eight

We Make It Happen

"There is no sure thing in work as in life, but the surest is the realization that we, ourselves, bear the responsibility for our own achievement."

Being a true professional has many implications. For example, it implies that we know what the substantive part of our job is and that we not only know how to do it, but that we do it to perfection. It also implies that we subordinates know the importance of having a positive relationship with our boss and that we take responsibility for making that relationship develop and prosper; and that we know that the source of our power is rooted in the trust and confidence that our boss holds for us.

There is an additional element which contributes to our professionalism that we must not overlook: we ourselves make it all happen. This is the most important secret of our subordinate role. The most important element of our making it happen for us is our own personal awareness. This kind of awareness not only involves having a clear understanding of ourselves—who we are, what makes us tick, and what we want to become—but also an awareness of our boss and the things that are happening that impact him, both positively and negatively. Some of the things the dynamic subordinate will be aware of are:

- Awareness of Our Behavior

We must understand our behavior. It is our behavior, more than anything else, that reveals us to other people. Motives can't be seen, and intentions can only be guessed; but what we do, how we act, and the way we talk can be described, and they carry important messages of our overt and implied meaning to others. These meanings impact the receivers either negatively or positively. We may be aware of some of these implied negative and hurtful meanings and may intend them for another person at times. Often, however, we do not mean to transmit negative messages, but they are perceived as such in the minds and emotions of the receivers because of our behavior. So our first challenge is to be aware of our behavior and its impact on others.

Do we behave in ways that arouse feelings of anger, hatred, frustration, fear, insecurity and distrust? To the extent that we generate these feelings in others, we are the catalyst of ineffective, inappropriate, and dysfunctional behavior in others.

When we hit someone's hot button (either deliberately or by accident), we are participating in and contributing to his inappropriate behavior. We must strive to act in a way as not to set in motion destructive and inept chains of behavior in others. Subordinates, especially, must recognize that congruent behavior is absolutely essential to their being effective in their jobs.

Only when we come to understand how we make others see and feel about us can we decide on how we need to change our behavior. For example, if my behavior consistently turns people off and creates negative emotions in them and I'm not aware of it, I'm living in a fool's paradise. I need to look at myself and find out what I am doing that causes negative responses so that I can decide how I need to change my behavior. This kind of awareness may only be possible if we listen to the feedback of a trusted friend, relative, or most especially a boss. These are the ones who have the data. We must help them to share it with us! But if our behavior has a negative effect on our boss, it is vital that we become aware of this information.

I was once told by a boss that the facial expressions that I made when he spoke not only made him nervous but also made him suspect that I disapproved of what he was saying. I was unaware of what I was doing. Suffice it to say that I took this feedback to heart and made it a policy to become more aware of what I was doing when, and why I was doing it. It was a most caring kind of feedback. It enhanced my own self-awareness.

- Awareness of Our Emotional/Rational Orientation

Some of us are driven more by emotions, and some of us are more pragmatic. Neither is intrinsically right or wrong; but either, depending on the situation, can be wrong or right.

When emotions of fear, greed, suspicion, and ambition are substituted in our decision-making process for fact, data, analysis and research, they are wrong. On the other hand, if we try to solve human problems that call for empathy, understanding, compassion, sympathy and care by using only logic, reason, and deduction, we are employing the wrong process to solve these issues. Unless we are fully aware of what we are doing, we may indeed victimize ourselves and others by our inappropriate behavior.

I have found that I tend to be emotionally oriented with a great impatience for considering facts, figures and hard data. Once, on the basis of my emotions, I sold a large block of stock that later increased tremendously in value. I had ignored looking at the hard data when I made my decision to sell and had allowed my emotions to carry the day. The lesson for me, of course, was to get someone with an understanding of hard data to help me with this kind of decision.

It is vitally important to us that we understand what our emotional/rational orientation is so that we can behave in ways that support the needs of our boss.

Once, when I was the leader of a company's team-building effort, one person displayed a deep and raging bitterness toward the organization for which he worked. His vitriolic attack rolled out like a volcano exploding; and like volcano ash, it covered the whole group with pessimism and negativism. It dampened the climate and put a wet blanket upon an otherwise positive occasion.

This was not a unique situation for him—he behaved this way in all settings. As a result, his boss was tired of him and his staff was concerned for him. He seemed to be unaware of the dreadful negative impact of his behavior on his own future. He was doing it all to himself.

- Awareness of Our Approach to Life

Our approach to life, people and situations can be positive or negative. On the negative side are fear, bitterness, cynicism, pessimism, suspicion, defensiveness and skepticism. On the positive side are optimism, patience, trust, good humor and love. Our behavior in large part flows from these kinds of powerful emotions, and almost inevitably we will impart to others the emotional flavor that motivates our own behavior. Negative behavior has about it an infectious emotional quality that quite often pollutes the feelings of an entire group.

Positive emotional orientation helps people and systems to function well — to trust, to enjoy, to take risks, to create, to move ahead, and to be more energetic. Negative emotions cause us to become defensive, wary, bitter and overly cautious. Our perceptions of people and situations are slanted, and the processes of thinking, problem-solving, and decision-making become polluted and dysfunctional.

My wife has been a victim of Alzheimer's disease for about ten years. Our lives have undergone a drastic change as a result. Those carefree golden years that we had planned have become our painful years! The challenge is there for me to face every day—"Don't be bitter. Don't let it make me bitter! Bitterness will only help to destroy the me that I am. So take it easy. Don't complain. Don't whine. See the bright side of things." And so I strive to make my approach to people and to life positive and cheerful. It isn't easy but it can be done!

- Awareness of Our Self-Concept

We need to understand and come to terms with our image of ourselves as a person — our self-concept.

There are some who hold a highly inflated view of themselves, their abilities, their talents and their merits. As a consequence, they are out of step with reality. They are not easy to be around. Equally as difficult are people, like myself, who see little good in themselves no matter what the external evidence may indicate to the contrary. For example, I was surprised when a certain group asked me to speak to them some years ago, astounded when they asked me to come back a second time, and incredulous about a third invitation!

This kind of disparity between our self-image and reality can greatly reduce our effectiveness with others, because it sparks negative reactions to us. I have a friend who always runs herself down with "poor me" statements. It is often painful and embarrassing to be around her. The more realistically we view ourselves, the better are our chances of being positive and effective.

In my own case, I have decided to take at face value the words and accolades of those who give me praise! If *they* believe it about me, why shouldn't *I*? Oh, of course I know all of those bad things about myself that others don't see, but I'll keep them buried! Maybe people know more about us than we think!

- Awareness of Our Vision of Our Future

A vision of what it is that we can become or would like to become is essential for our growth and development. We must have an image of how we want to change, to grow, and to be. The motivation for this growth must come from within — nobody can force us to take charge of ourselves. Our future is created by our efforts to reach the star to which we have attached our vision.

How much do we each value our lives? What road do we want to travel and what do we want our lives to mean? What do we want to achieve, and how will we do it? Effective people create their vision and then find the ways and means for making it reality. It is part of the self-fulfilling prophecy concept —dream it and it will come true!

In 1954 I was an administrative officer in the U.S. Embassy in Rome, Italy. There I dared to dream—to plan—to envisage that I would one day hold the highest administrative position in the Department of State in Washington, Deputy Under Secretary of State for Administration.

I worked, studied, planned, created win/win networks and, in 1965, eleven years later, the dream was realized. I was appointed to that post by President Kennedy. Dreams can come true!

It is strange how this vision concept works. My son, Robert, was not interested in athletics for most of the years of his life. No football, basketball, tennis or golf for him! In college his participation was only at the required level. Then, by some process of which neither of us is fully aware, he became interested in the newly emerging sport of the triathlon race. It is a grueling athletic event consisting of swimming 1 mile, biking 22 miles and running 7 miles. His vision was to win that event for his age group. This vision was the catalyst for a very rigid daily routine of swimming, biking, and running. He did not allow himself to be discouraged or dissuaded in his goal. He swam, he biked and he ran. He raced and he raced and he raced! Then, on May 14, 1989, his goal was achieved; his vision was realized. He won the triathlon for his age group at the Phoenix International Bud Light U.S. Triathlon Series!

Whatever the direction of our vision, if we are dedicated enough we can make it come true!

- Awareness of Our Values

We need to define our ethical values. What are the hard and fast expectations that we hold for the things that we do, that others do, or that society does for and to people? What are our organizational responsibilities toward our environment, toward safety, toward honesty, toward openness, and toward society itself? Do we ever find ourselves doing things "in a role" or "in response to the boss" that violate our own value system? And how do we excuse that behavior? How do we rationalize our behavior so that we don't feel guilty? Do we claim that we love our family, yet continuously neglect them because of our work—perhaps as a result of our compulsive, workaholic nature? How do we rationalize this?

One of the results of our self-search can be more relevance between our theories and our behavior, and more congruence between the values we hold and the things we do.

- Awareness of Our Own Needs

We should be aware of the extent to which we have become the slave of our own needs. Theory holds that we all have four great psychological needs: survival (security), love (belonging), potency (influence), and ego (self-esteem). While we are all different in the degree to which we feel these needs, we are the same in that, if we don't watch ourselves, we can become driven by one or more of these needs to achieve the ends that, we hope, will fulfill them. When we arrive at this "driven" state, we may become unthinking, irrational slaves of the need(s). We then are no longer free.

What is the status of your needs? How much of your activity centers around getting these needs fulfilled? How does it affect the other areas of your life? Other people in your life?

Sometimes people's need for power, for ego satisfaction and for money can drive them to take foolish risks—perhaps even illegal ones. The stock market and Savings & Loan scandals of recent years provide tragic examples of this kind of behavior.

• Awareness of Our Obligation to Assume Responsibility for Ourselves and What We Are

Until quite recently, I had thought that the ways that I felt about people and situations were the result of internal forces over which I had no control, let alone choice. In like manner, I thought my behavior, no matter how ineffective and illogical it might seem when based entirely upon emotional stimuli, was also but a natural outgrowth of my feelings, which were spontaneous reactions to others. Since it was all quite automatic, I thought myself to be the hapless victim of the behavior of others. "*You* make me mad." "*You* frustrate me." "It is *your* fault that I behave as I do." "*You* started it."

This acceptance of my feelings as being automatic reflexes within me triggered all kinds of harsh behavior toward others, such as
— retaliatory behavior because of the hurts they caused.
— angry behavior because people didn't see things my way.
— competitive behavior. I wanted to win.
— harsh behavior to punish what seemed to be a disregard for me and my ideas.

It was not until quite late in my life that I came to realize that my feelings are not necessarily automatic; they are of my own choosing! Over time, I learned that the ways that I feel are actually up to me. I make the choice. I realized, too, that I also have a choice about how I will behave in any given situation.

The catalyst for my new understanding was an intense encounter-group experience in the early 60's when my wife and I participated in

114 We Make It Happen

T-groups (training groups), she in one, I in another.

Verla, my wife, came from a family where feelings were expressed freely, and she herself is very direct and very open. She says candidly what she thinks and feels. When I was in the State Department, I used to tell her, "We're in the diplomatic service and you aren't very diplomatic. You will ruin my career!" She would say, "I only speak honestly and I simply give answers when people ask me for information. I really think that people like me and trust me." I responded, "Verla, I'm the expert in this business, so do it my way."

I came from a family that behaved very indirectly in their relationships with each other. Direct statements were considered being impolite and to cause hurt feelings. As a result, people in my family resorted to hinting and implying and assuming. There was a lot of time spent in such speculation as "I wonder what she really meant when she said ...."; or "'a' said this and 'b' said that, and 'c' responded thusly, so this must mean that 'e'!"

After about the third day at the T-Group, Verla said, "The women are telling me nice things. They say that I come across as being honest, sincere and caring, and that they really trust me."

"That's nice," I replied, "My group isn't telling me that."

"What feedback are you getting?"

"The men are telling me that I am indirect and don't commit myself on any issue. That I have a lot of fancy theories. That I think I am better than they and that they sure don't trust me and wouldn't want to work for me!"

I was both confused and hurt by their data! Finally I asked, "How do you get these impressions of me? What am I doing that causes you to see me in this light? How can I, poor old shy, lonely Bill, who feels so much less self-worth than all of you, be seen as feeling superior?"

They said, "Because of the ways you act. Your shyness and loneliness don't show at all. You don't act like you want to become one of us. You don't go to the bar. You don't enter our activities. You always have fancy theories about everything. You don't act like you really like us. You come across as being arrogant and conceited."

I was stunned!

Then it began to dawn on me—my shyness was causing me to seem haughty and aloof! While my behavior was motivated by my fears, the meanings that my behavior carried to others was entirely different! My God! During all those "shy years," had I been telling people by my behavior that I felt superior to them?

I consulted a psychologist friend about how I might change my feelings. He said, "Do you have about $3000 you can spare for some sessions with me?"

"No way," was my reply.

He said, "Okay. First you must take responsibility for the way that you behave. You have a choice: you can allow your behavior to be motivated by your feelings; or your behavior can be motivated by your intellect. Make the choice!

"Second, behave as you want to be seen — the way that you would become."

"What do you mean by that?" I asked.

"Well, tell me some ways that you would like for people to feel about you."

I replied, "I would like them to feel that
— I'm friendly.
— I'm warm.
— I'm honest.
— I care.
— I'm not superior or arrogant.
— I'm sincere and genuine.
— I'm fun."

"Okay," he said, "now start acting those ways! Be friendly to the people that you meet, even strangers. Take an interest in them so that they will see that you do care and that you are a warm, thoughtful person. Show that you are sincere and genuine by the things that you do for them. Behave as you would become to them! You have a choice in the behavior that you select, so exercise that choice deliberately! Don't put your behavior on the 'automatic pilot' of your feelings, but stand firmly at the controls. You be responsible for all that you say and do."

"But," I protested, "I'm shy — I may not feel like behaving those ways!"

He said, "I'm sure that you won't feel like it, especially in the beginning. But you don't like the results of your shy behavior, so try acting in some different ways. Put your head in control of you behavior for a change!"

That conversation was a revelation to me. I realized I was responsible for the things that I had heretofore thought of as being automatic and unalterable. All at once I realized that it was I who had been making the choices all along on how I felt. The buck stopped with me!

I am responsible for the ways that I feel.

I am responsible for my actions and words and behavior; and I must accept the full consequences for the feelings in others that my behavior produces.

- Awareness of How We Relate to Others

I must realize that the important others in my life may be very different from me in many ways, and this doesn't make them either bad or wrong. It simply means that they may approach a particular situation from a different perspective.

We can't assume that our own perception of a situation is the same as another's. We can take no relationship for granted! Just because a relationship looks okay to us does not mean that it is all right with the other person. People are able to hide their feelings so that no one else knows that they are dissatisfied with a relationship. Such a situation can go along for years before it explodes and comes to a violent end.

We had long-standing family friends who had been married 35 years when the man quite suddenly broke off the marital relationship. They had three lovely children and a beautiful home. He was successful in a professional practice. The wife was seemingly loving and supportive, as had been the husband. There was no other man or other woman involved. There wasn't a clue that we could find in reviewing our relationship with them over the years to make us suspect his unhappiness. Yet, on New Year's Day after a gala New Year's Eve celebration, he packed his things, moved out and filed for divorce. To this day, neither family nor friends have ever discovered the source of his discontent. We were all deceived by surface harmony.

All relationships must be constantly nurtured if they are to remain healthy. Managing and maintaining a healthy relationship is like keeping the Brooklyn bridge well painted— the effort must be continuous. The painters can never stop. If relationships are to remain solid and positive, they must be worked at constantly. The little hurts, bruises and misunderstandings of each personal encounter must be attended to — examined, explained and solved with explanations and apologies —at once! If they aren't, they can, like a tiny cut, fester, enlarge and produce a raging fever. Do not take any relationship that you value for granted! To do so is to risk losing it.

We must remember that it is not the big problems, the big differences or the dramatic issues which so often cause our relationships to fail. The biggest irritants, over time, are the little things that we do, say, or fail to do or say to each other day after day: inconsiderate behavior that carries the message that you don't have me much on your mind; thoughtless comments which convey the meaning that you don't really care how I feel; small cruel acts that tell me that you want to punish me, to get even, and to hurt me rather than to love me; words left unspoken, like "I love you" or "I appreciate" or "thanks for helping"; words and phrases that constantly put me down and carry the meaning to me that you think I'm an incompetent dummy; the many ways that you treat me as if I were a child whom you must always remind, always admonish, always scold; the little things that must always be done your way, thus forcing your ways of life on me, such as the way we go to church, where we sit in a restaurant, etc.

None of these things are very important in and of themselves. Certainly none of them are worth causing a divorce; but if allowed to go on over a long period of time, they will erode the closest and most secure relationship.

All of these little irritating problems are quite easily cured, granting four important ifs:

if the parties concerned truly wish a good relationship to exist.

if the parties are willing to look honestly at themselves or are willing to get honest feedback about themselves in order to see what they are doing.

if the parties are willing to make the necessary changes,

if the parties are willing to make this kind of exploration and renewal an ongoing process— forever.

Beaming our antennas in the direction of others is a very important art which is too infrequently practiced. We all seem to be so taken up with "self" that we have little time or patience for others.

- Awareness of Our Boss

To be successful, however, the subordinate.must be alert to what is going on inside those around him, especially his boss. This is true because the subordinate's ability to serve the needs of his boss is uniquely dependent upon the subordinate's accurate understanding of his boss. We have already discussed this, but it is so important that it bears repetition: we must know what our boss values. The basic expectations of the boss (awareness of what the boss values) is also sometimes difficult to get at. If all else fails, ask!

On the other side of the coin and equally important, the subordinate must be aware of the boss's perception of her/him, including behavior which the boss is indifferent to or actively dislikes . This sort of insight is not easy to obtain, but it is so vital that we must consider it to be a primary objective. Again, if all else fails, ask!

Finally, if we can achieve an awareness of the psychological needs of our boss, we have the key to making ourselves valuable to the boss over the long term, for we can work in ways that will insure that his needs are being met. This awareness will come only if we listen carefully to what our boss says, observe his reactions to events and situations, learn his moods and their causes, and intently study him as a person. If we are sensitive, observant and patient, this awareness will come to us!

CONCLUSION

To make our relationships with important others solid and positive, we must seek out and destroy the petty, recurring irritants that endanger the relationship. We must stop doing the things we know or suspect are annoying to others, and we must put in perspective the things that others are doing to us which we find exasperating. Our thoughts and behavior must reflect our priorities!

How do we go about doing this? To put the above prescription into practice, I think we must do four things:

First, we must learn as much as we can about the dynamics of human relationships. This means that we learn about some of the things that go on within us and within others. This I call "Awareness of Basic Life Forces."

Second, we must come to a full and honest understanding and acceptance of ourselves, our positive qualities as well as our negatives.

Third, we must accept the full and absolute responsibility for whatever we do, whatever the reason. No matter what the perceived provocation might be, we are responsible for the ways that we act.

Finally and above all else, we must graciously, unselfishly and deliberately put the needs of our boss ahead of our own, whatever those needs happen to be. This may be the single hardest thing for the dynamic subordinate to do, but it is also the most important. In doing this, he garners the gratitude and trust of his boss. Putting the needs of our boss ahead of our own needs is indeed the consummate art. This is the unselfish act of a truly dynamic subordinate. And this is the stuff of which successful leader-managers are made. It is the most potent secret that the subordinate holds.

Conclusion

Dynamic subordinancy is the essence of all sustained and powerful leadership. The secrets of the dynamic subordinate are many, and every successful subordinate knows them and practices them. The key is for the leader-manager to remember them from his own subordinancy experiences and to assiduously practice them in his own relationships with his boss.

A number of the unique concepts-secrets that the dynamic subordinate understands and actualizes in his work that distinguish him from the ordinary subordinate are worth reviewing.

• First, there is the concept of the dual nature of the subordinate's role — subordinate/leader-manager. The dynamic subordinate attends to these two roles in some very special ways.

• The dynamic subordinate recognizes that his leadership-managerial role is one of the most important facets in building the trust of his boss. Therefore, he doesn't just do the job; he does it the way he knows his boss wants it done. He does the things that his boss values. He accepts the concept that it is the boss who owns the job and that it is the boss who ultimately decides the job's "what, when, and how." The dynamic subordinate seeks to carry out his boss's expressed perception of the job so perfectly that his boss will swell with pride and satisfaction.

• The dynamic subordinate creates a positive and trusting relationship with his boss. He does not overlook nor minimize the importance of his role as a subordinate.

Such a relationship is fostered by the ways that the subordinate does his work, as described above. But creating a positive and trusting relationship involves even more subtle and substantive activities. All too often, the leader-manager falls into the fatal trap of thinking that as long as the job gets done, nothing else matters to his boss. A dynamic subordinate understands the importance of

— knowing and meeting the emotional needs of his boss. The boss must have confidence in the subordinate's loyalty and honesty as well as in the quality of his work; the boss must feel a sense of belonging and a sense of power which, in turn, will enhance his self-image.

— knowing and fulfilling the expectations of his boss. This means constructing a profile of his boss so he knows what makes him tick: what his hot buttons are; what makes him growl and what makes him purr; what turns him on and what turns him off; and how he operates as a person It is only with such knowledge that a subordinate can successfully meet his boss's expectations.

— making sure that, in his responses to his boss, he never gives off verbal or nonverbal vibes that indicate defensiveness or retaliation. The dynamic subordinate avoids any action or reaction that could put doubt into the boss's mind concerning his loyalty, professionalism, and total commitment to the boss's welfare and success. For example, the dynamic subordinate never publicly disagrees with his boss, never criticizes him, and never keeps his boss in the dark about what he is doing and planning.

— giving the boss credit for the successful accomplishment of jobs in his area of responsibility, extolling the boss's virtues upward to *his* boss, taking the blame for whatever goes wrong, and above all else, expressing pride in the success of the boss.

The dynamic subordinate who does these things will be empowered to fulfill his own needs—he can safely exercise initiative and pursue innovation. He must take every opportunity to fulfill the dual nature of his role, first as subordinate and then as leader-manager, thus enhancing both in the eyes of his boss.

• The dynamic subordinate must attend to his own mental and physical well-being. As we have seen, his is an arduous and complicated task which requires toughness and self-discipline. A healthy mind and body result from the self-discipline that enables the subordinate to have time for his family and for his own personal physical well-being. These provide the foundation for an inner serenity which sustains every successful man and woman.

• An external support system, composed of friends and colleagues in other parts of the organization and in other organizations across the country, is essential to the dynamic subordinate. He will need this group to fall back on in times of adversity. It is the security blanket that nurtures his self-confidence.

The contents of this book have sprung from my own long experience as a subordinate/leader-manager. They are things that I have learned from serving powerful and important people. The lessons that I have drawn from these experiences—the secrets of dynamic subordinancy—may seem obvious to any intelligent individual, but subordinates at all levels quite regularly disregard these truths. The public record shows that many high-level leader-managers fail to heed them, often with disastrous results. *Newsweek* described Armand Hammer as "the 92-year-old oil tycoon, wheeler-dealer, friend of Soviet leaders since Lenin, adviser to princes and presidents." In July 1990, Mr. Hammer, chief of Occidental Petroleum, faced a stockholder suit that questioned the propriety of his use of company funds to help build The Armand Hammer Museum of Art and Cultural Center in Los Angeles. Mr. Hammer apparently forgot (if he ever knew) that he also was a subordinate, notwithstanding his great wealth and power. Like subordinates everywhere, he seemingly forgot or ignored the fact that he must pursue goals that his boss (in this case, the stockholders) valued, before he could safely pursue his own. Since he didn't do this, he faced their wrath.

These "secrets" work the same in the realm of political leadership. The world and the world's great causes need enlightened and far-sighted leadership; but when the visions of the leader are not valued by his boss (the voters), the leader loses his power. Winston Churchill, Jimmy Carter, Margaret Thatcher, and LBJ are examples of leaders who somehow failed to build the bank of trust with their constituencies that would keep them in power.

The world needs leaders who are inspired with great visions for the common good, but it also needs leaders who can retain their positions and power long enough to see their visions become reality. The basis for this kind of leadership lies in the ability of subordinates, even subordinates who are presidents and prime ministers, to create and sustain strong, positive relationships with the bosses (people) of the world; for it is they who are the sources of all legitimate power. The leader-manager/subordinate who comprehends the nature of such relationships and acts accordingly understands the importance of dynamic subordinancy, i.e., that dynamic subordinancy is the essence of sustained and powerful leadership. This is the ultimate secret of dynamic subordinancy.

The End

Appendix

Understanding Human Nature

The following eight basic concepts of human relations are of critical importance to any subordinate in relating to his/her boss. These eight essays are part of the CABS *The Human Relations Letter* series that is published bimonthly.

1. Our Two Worlds
2. Our Emotions
3. Our Expectations
4. Our Process
5. Our Incongruent Behavior
6. The Law of Reciprocal Behavior
7. Our Needs
8. Self-Interest

For more information, please see the order form in the back of the book.

THE HUMAN RELATIONS LETTER

Dedicated to the Art of Creating Effective Relationships

Issue #1

OUR TWO WORLDS

Our Pattern of Thinking and Talking That Affects Us and Our
Relationships With Others

● **Introduction**

As human beings, we live our lives in two distinct worlds—one of
fact and certainty and one of emotions and ambiguity. The world of
certainty is that part of our lives which deals with objects and our
rational side—our thing world. Our world of ambiguity deals with
people and our feeling or emotional side—our human world. One
might be called our hard-data world and the other our soft-data world.
They might look like this:

This concept holds special significance for all of us because it is one
of the basic concepts underlying effective communications and successful
human relationships.

● **Our Hard-Data World**

Our certain world, or hard-data world, is one of finite facts and
scientifically measured situations. It is a comfortable world because we
can be sure of and confident with our answers. They are right and we
can depend on them staying right. This world is rational, ordered,
secure—and thus helps to fulfill one of our most basic human needs—
the need for security.

In this certain world, we can measure a cubic centimeter of blood
and know that it will always be the same amount and know how that
amount relates to other activities and functions we must perform with
it and around it. We measure our temperature and count our heart beats
and know that both are scientific, accurate, and sure. We know our
weight by a scale that measures us in pounds; we calculate our waist-
lines in inches; and at the end of the month we receive an accurately
computed paycheck made out in dollars.

And for all our lives we will be involved with, respond to and feel comfortable about living in a world of scientifically accurate hard-data facts—speed limits, bank accounts, house payments, light bills and hosts of other measurable facts.

Another part of this certain world is that it is ordered into dependable, scientifically proven cause-and-effect relationships. Each unit of effort can be measured, and its effect upon other things can be predicted and depended on. We are assured of the consequences. The feedback is direct, swift and dependable. For example, if I write too many checks, I will run out of money and my checks will bounce. If I drive too fast, the police will pick me up and I'll get a ticket. If I eat too much too often, I'll get fat. The results are fact and come in measurable forms. And this simplifies life for all of us, for then we don't have to wonder and worry and think—we know! A large portion of our daily lives at work and at home is so ordered, like the laws of gravity, into a dependable routine of absolute cause and effect. And this is good, for we can and do feel secure within it.

● **Our Soft-Data World**

There is also a vast part of our world that is uncharted and made up of emotions and ambiguity. This might be called our soft-data world. In this world there is little, if any, real fact and rationality, and there is no dependable cause-and-effect relationship. In this world there are few absolutes and many uncertainties. And in this uncertain world, the answers don't even remain constant—for just when we think we understand our relationship with another person, it may change.

This uncertain world involves our association with all other human beings—bosses, subordinates, spouses, peers, children, parents, friends and even enemies. And this misty world of ambiguity will always encompass a major portion of our lives. This is our very own private world.

Yet, when one stops to think about it, for all of its uncertainty and ambiguity, this world is most important to each of us, for it is our human world. It is the world of our feelings—the world of tears, love, laughter and fun—the world of our longings and yearnings to become better and achieve more. This is the world of *self*—the world of *others* and the world that is the relationship of these two. This is the world of our judgments, our estimates of the future and our evaluation of ourselves as well as of others. This is our very own personal world that no one else can share or be a part of unless and until we let them in.

But the fact is that despite our sophistication in communications, our fine educations, our great technology, our logic and rationality, we, as individual human beings, have difficulty finding certainty and fact and real security in either of our worlds, for they often impinge upon each other. This is partially the result of the distortions and ambiguities that are at work in our human world and partially the result of our failure to really communicate with each other correctly or accurately.

● **Differences Between the Two**

— In our hard-data world, knowledge is finite and definite, so it is cumulative. The learnings of the centuries are available to us all. We learn our hard-data facts intellectually and we store our knowledge in books, in libraries, and in computers.

— In our soft-data world, knowledge is not cumulative. This is the world of uncharted waters that we must traverse almost blindly. We each must learn how to be people and relate to others exactly as did Adam. In this world we learn experientially—from our mistakes and failures as well as from our successes—over the short span of our own lifetimes.

— In the hard-data world things are either right or wrong, better or best, and everything in it has its own standard and value which all agree upon. In this world there are few differences, for the nature of the data rules out differences. So it's appropriate to use hard verbs and adjectives because they refer to the absolute nature of the data, i.e., is, are, right, wrong, better, best, fastest, strongest, etc.

— In the soft-data world there are few rights and wrongs. Nothing has an absolute value. Beauty is in the eye of the beholder. In this world it is appropriate to use only soft verbs—I see, I feel, I believe, I perceive, I need, etc.—because the data is what each individual perceives it to be for himself/herself. The fact of perception is only our own way of seeing things and what we see, and may not be held by anybody else!! And since all people are different, this is a very, very complex world, filled with ambiguity and uncertainty and infinite differences.

— In the hard-data world, we have problems to solve. A problem is a hard-data situation out of tolerance which needs fixing. We Americans are great problem-solvers, and our hard-data worlds abound with problems to solve and problems which have been successfully solved. Putting a man on the moon is a good illustration of a brilliant hard-data performance.

— There are really no problems in our soft-data world. The world of human likes, perceptions, needs, wants, etc., is so widely different and mutually contradictory as to have no hard-data solutions. For example, if I am cold and you are hot in the same room, and neither of us will change the way we are clothed, there may be no hard-data solution for the predicament. It is a dilemma—because there is no solution. To be sure, we can agree to accommodate one at the expense of the other, or we may make a compromise that satisfies neither.

— Dilemmas also occur when a person or a group has such strongly-held emotions (anger, hurt, hate, etc.—due to violated principles of all kinds) that the opposing factions will not even talk to each other, let alone come to some sort of compromise. The problems of the Middle East, Northern Ireland, and some labor/management disputes illustrate harsh human dilemmas without real and lasting solutions.

● **Deep Relationships Are of the Soft Data World**

As intellectually and rationally oriented as the hard-data world is and as well as we have learned to manipulate that hard-data world, still people's deep relationships with each other—both positive and negative—are of the soft-data world. The reality of us (people) is more in our soft-data feelings about ourselves and our perceptions of others than it is in our hard-data bank of intellectual facts. The subtle meanings that others attribute to what we say and how we act is the soft data about us. And it is private until others are willing to trust us with it.

People don't and won't really know each other unless and until they can talk soft-data talk—human talk—to each other and listen and empathize and sympathize about—

— their mutual concerns
— their mutual hurts
— their mutual disappointments
— their mutual lives' tragedies
— their mutual defeats
— their mutual hopes and dreams
— their mutual frustrations
— their mutual victories
— their mutual fears
— their mutual fantasies
— themselves in depth as real, live human beings

However, people won't talk to each other in these ways until there is a deep feeling of mutual trust. But strange as it seems, when people begin to talk to each other in these ways, trust starts to grow, people become closer, and life has more meaning. We can't really know each other until we share some of our soft data. It is our soft-data world that is the world of joy, of sorrow, of tears, of love,—of people.

● **Soft Data Rules the World of People**

All kinds of hard-data symbols of power and wealth—armies, air forces, factories, farm production, exports, money in circulation, health standards, standards of living, etc., are used to measure the status of the countries of the world. These are things that we can see and count and measure, and if they are held by an unfriendly power, they can cause us to be afraid. However, it is soft data—our emotions—that galvanize us into action. When we become so totally angry and frustrated, and feel so deprived of the things that we value that we can't contain ourselves any longer, we burst into action.

We have seen this happening in one iron curtain country after another as they fearlessly face all of the hard-data destructive power that their authoritarian masters could muster. The soft data of the people has easily overthrown the hard-data power of the dictators.

The sad and frightening aspect of this is that our soft data can be negative as well as positive, and in many cases it would seem that our negative soft-data worlds of anger, hate, and vindictiveness is the more powerful of the two. North Ireland, South Africa and the Middle East are three examples of rampant negative soft data with there being little possibility for change.

● **The Business World**

The business world (as life itself) is, in reality, a subtle mixture of both hard and soft data. In business as in life, hard data has its limits.

Most aspects of the future—the future results of today's decisions—reflect our judgments and our expectations of the future. They are soft data—unproven and unprovable in advance Thus much of what happens in the business world is based upon human judgments (which are soft data).

Likewise, every decision that a group of people has to make may involve some conflict, because people probably will have differing viewpoints, feelings, ideas and judgments of the future, based upon the same hard-data facts.

Decisions that involve judgment fall somewhere to the right of the hard-data line.

HARD
DATA
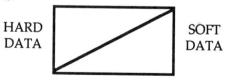
SOFT
DATA

A hard-data decision (such as the thousands of decisions that had to be made in the process of putting a man on the moon) may be as simple as making sure that all of the hard-data facts are in and support the decision. The tragic disaster in our space program was a case where people, for various reasons, failed to properly evaluate the hard-data facts and overrode that hard data with their own soft-data judgments! In some cases, however, there may be only a few facts available, with the decision depending on the insight, experience and judgment of the decision-makers. The farther the right on the continuum that a decision falls, the more ambiguity and uncertainty there will be in that decision.

In life as well as in business, this is a tough area for us because it puts such a high premium on our own judgment, and inevitably these decisions take on some of our own emotional bias. We can never be sure of the validity and accuracy of our soft-data inputs until we know the outcome. This also makes it possible for others with their own soft-data differences or with the advantage of hindsight, to ask, "Why did you do it that way?" Such decisions are often referred to as "judgment calls," which can be extremely risky for the people who must make them. In these situations, the more open all of those involved can be about their soft-data—i.e., their reasons, perceptions, their fears, concerns, etc., behind the decision—the more helpful we will be to others making these kinds of decisions and the better the decisions are likely to be.

HARD DATA		SOFT DATA
TO PUT A SPACESHIP IN ORBIT		TO CURE THE POVERTY CYCLE IN AN AREA

● **Our Personal (Individual) Orientation**

As we would expect, knowing how different we all are, we each have a different place on which we fall on the hard-data/soft-data continuum.

Some of us are very "external" people (extroverts) who see things in black-and white terms, are intellectual, rational and data-oriented. Some of us who are more introverted, on the other hand, tend to be more soft-data oriented. We are more emotional in the way we make our decisions, relate to people and live our lives. Neither position can be said to be either right or wrong, but it's well that we know ourselves so that we can be more effective in the things that we have to do. If I am called upon to comfort a friend whose mother has died, I don't give much help by talking logic and reason. On the other hand, my emotions provide a poor basis on which to make my judgments regarding buying and selling my stocks!!

So, if I happen to fall into the soft-data world, I will be well-served to seek out some hard-data people to help me with my hard-data decisions.

● **Jobs**

The hard-data concept is important for a boss and subordinate because the more hard-data, results-oriented a job is or can be defined as being, the easier it is for a subordinate to do it and the easier it is for the boss to evaluate the effectiveness of the subordinate in getting the job done. Hard data is the opposite of ambiguity, so the wise subordinate and the wise boss will translate as much of the job's ambiguity as they can into hard data. Similarly, the wise boss will translate as much of his instructions, policies, processes, objectives, descriptions, etc., into hard data as he possibly can. He will leave as little as possible to conjecture.

I had a boss once who told me, when I asked him what my job was, "Just live up to the horizons of your responsibility!" This is soft data at its worst.

There is an excellent process for getting jobs defined in hard-data terms that is called "management by objectives." This concept asks that each boss and subordinate define, *in hard-data terms*, the five to ten results the subordinate will achieve over discrete periods of time. In this way, the boss and the subordinate have established a contract in hard-data terms of what is expected. Since it is hard data, it can be evaluated by hard-data standards.

● **Relationships**

Our soft-data worlds are just as real, vital and meaningful to us as are our hard-data worlds. It's just that we haven't had much experience talking about ourselves around our soft data and, as a result, we are in the habit of talking as if all data were hard data. We say such things as—

"It is cold in here."

"That is a beautiful painting."

"Bush is a great president."

None of this is hard data, yet we have made it sound hard by the way we have expressed ourselves. If we could learn to express our soft-data in soft-data terms, i.e., "I *think* Bush is a great president," then if we disagree, we can discuss our differences and our reasons. Maybe we could even find a middle ground of agreement! We would no longer have to argue or fight!

We must try to make sure that, in every relationship and in every encounter, we define the what, why, when, where, and how of each and every expectation and every soft-data concept that we have expressed so that this soft data becomes hard reality for us. If we will first acknowledge the fact that we are in a soft-data area, we then can come to agreement on the hard-data criteria that we can use to evaluate what we differ about.

Conflict in the hard-data world can usually be quite easily and quite readily solved, and solved without creating too many emotional negatives. In the hard-data world, we "get the facts"! And if they are really facts—not opinions and not judgments—then all of us will pretty much agree on a common answer. There is no room for *differences* in facts alone!!

But—when we move just a bit to the past *causes* of those facts (judgments), or to the future meanings of those facts (intuition and judgment), or to what to do or not do as a result of those facts (decisions), then conflicts can and often do occur. We see things differently, and it is this seeing-things-differently wherein lies the source of much human conflict.

It isn't just the fact that we may differ that is the source of our conflict. Our real conflict often occurs when we not only insist on the rightness of our own point of view, but we also insist that the other must accept our way as well!

Much of the harsh and unremitting conflict that besets the human race is the result of our many soft-data differences and the way we elect to handle them. They become win/lose contests:

—I want things this way.
   —You want them that way.
—I like my food this way.
   —You like yours that way.
—I want order in my life.
   —You like things flexible
—I want to be alone.
   —You want people.
—I think we should sell.
   —You think we should buy.
—I want to go here.
   —You want to go there.
—I think it's better to do it this way.
   —You think it's better that way.
—I believe in a strong military.
   —You see it as a threat to peace.
—I like Mr. X as president.
   —You support Mr. Y.
—I remember the situation this way.
   —You recall it that way.
The arguments go on and on and on!
   • No one is absolutely right!
   • No one is absolutely wrong!

• There is no proof positive that either position is right or wrong, better or best!

When these kinds of soft-data conflicts occur, we often become very selfish about our own point of view and our self-interests, so that we insist that things get decided and/or done in a way that satisfies us. There seems to be no willingness to compromise—it is all or nothing! And when we get our way by force or by other means, the other party to the conflict is left feeling very dissatisfied! One wins and the other loses.

Such losses are often not taken lightly nor accepted as being final. And it is not unusual for such situations to turn into physical violence with tragic results; or if physical violence is not the result, there can be such extreme feelings of anger and hostility expressed in hurtful ways that the relationship is permanently ruptured.

These outcomes are not unusual in families, work situations, and with ethnic groups within countries.

● **Organizational Meanings**

In order for a complex organization to function smoothly, with each department relating to the other departments in collaboration and support, and with people pursuing a common purpose, there must be a solid base of hard-data information concerning missions, goals, policies, standards, ethics, procedures, jobs, power, expectations, etc. The more ambiguity that exists in a complex organization, the more likely it is that there will be overlap of duties, confusion, contradiction, dissension and ineffectiveness. Managers must not tolerate or suffer such a situation to exist. If we are to be successful in a job, we must take the initiative to insure that we and others are operating from a foundation of shared hard data: what each job is; what each job does; how each job relates; how each job is done; what are each job's end products, etc. The person with the power has the responsibility for making this the case in his/her area of responsibility.

● **Summary**

OUR TWO WORLDS

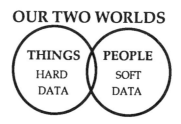

THINGS | PEOPLE

HARD | SOFT

DATA | DATA

Facts	<—>	Perceptions
LogicReason	<—>	Instinct, Opinion
Cause & Effect	<—>	None
Certain	<—>	Ambiguous
Absolute	<—>	Conjectural
Same	<—>	Different
Rational	<—>	Emotional
Measurable	<—>	Infinite
Objective	<—>	Subjective
Scientific	<—>	Intuitive
Right, Wrong	<—>	Complex
Black, White	<—>	Gray
Use Hard-Data	<—>	Use Soft-Data
Verbs!		Verbs!
Uniformity	<—>	Variety
Agreement	<—>	Conflict
Problems	<—>	Dilemmas
Solutions	<—>	No Solutions

● **Discussion Questions**

1.   Please think of a situation that went awry because the hard-data facts were not made explicit. What were the consequences? What were the learnings? Please describe.
2.   Please think of a situation that was almost entirely a soft-data decision. How was the decision made? How did it turn out? What could have been done better?
3.   Why are the situations that fall chiefly in the soft-data world so prone to conflict? Describe such an experience. How could it have been done better? What were the learnings?
4.   Did you ever work in a complex organization where there was so much ambiguity that no one knew for sure just how to get things done? What were some of the consequences. Please describe.
5.   How does the careless use of hard-data verbs to describe a soft-data situation affect you? Describe. What can be done about it?
6.   How can we make sure, in our discussions leading up to decisions, that it is clear where we and others are coming from, i.e., hard data (facts) or soft data (ideas, needs, emotions, etc.)? What difference might it make? Describe an experience.
7.   What are some ways that husbands and wives, parents and children, bosses and subordinates, can use this hard-data/soft-data concept to improve the quality of their communications, the quality of their

relationships, and the quality of their decisions? Please discuss and describe.

8.   How can we make sure that the decisions we reach in meetings and with each other are as hard-data oriented as possible, i.e., that each person is absolutely sure of the what, when, why, how, and who that apply to him? Please discuss.

9.   Thinking about some of your own important relationships, do you find that there are serious differences between you? How do you handle them? Have you ever lost a friend as a result of how your differences were handled? Please think about how you do deal with your differences with others.

10. What is something else, not mentioned above, that might be discussed for the benefit of better relationships? Please describe it and discuss it.

Bill Crockett

THE HUMAN RELATIONS LETTER
Dedicated to the Art of Creating Effective Relationships

Issue #5

OUR EMOTIONS

● Introduction

We all have emotions – all people, both men and women, young and old, have emotions. They are invisible but powerful forces in human affairs. Feelings come as part of our standard equipment, and they can be either positive or negative. We hold feelings about people and situations as well as about ourselves. Yet our emotions aren't a part of our involuntary system – we can control and make decisions about our emotions.

● Triggering Events

Our lives are filled with triggering events, things that impact us emotionally: a sick child, a car's dead battery, highway congestion, a late report, a cross boss, a new job, a strange situation, etc. We are bombarded by these events every day of our lives. A triggering event is the action of people or an act of nature or an act of God, or even something within ourselves that puts stress and pressure on us and causes us to feel either positive or negative. Every minute all day long, from the time that we awake until sleep overtakes us, there is an endless bombardment of events that trigger our emotions either positively or negatively. As a result, we can become a volatile bundle of pent-up emotions just waiting for one more incident to cause us to explode.

● Some Emotional Facts

First, our feelings are invisible to other human beings unless we elect to share them. For many reasons, we often prefer to hide what we really feel, and we often pretend to feel something else, especially if our feelings are negative. We keep our real feelings invisible. Sometimes we inadvertently give others a clue as to how we feel by the ways that we talk and act; but when we are confronted about this, we often deny feeling those ways!

Second, feelings are the device we humans use to evaluate any situation or relationship of which we are a part. We stick with people and things that we like, enduring many hardships in the process, because we like them. And we will leave what seems to be an ideal situation because, for some reason, we don't like it. Our feelings about a person or situation is our measurement device.

Third, feelings are one of the most powerful motivational forces in all human affairs – one-on-one, work groups, organizations, nations, etc. And when these feelings are negative, involving such things as hate, lust, vengeance, anger, suspicion, greed, etc., they can lead to dreadful consequences. When these negative forces get started, they tend to perpetuate themselves; they are infectious and cancerous! This proclivity of the human being is what I call "The Law of the Negative Force." Negative forces feed on the past and tend to convert every activity into a negative. Once in motion, the negative force in a relationship is very hard to get turned back into the positive.

Fourth, we have what I call our emotional hangovers (hold-overs). This is true of both positive as well as negative feelings, but it is the negative that cause us the most problems.

When events cause us stress and the rise of our emotional temperature, we generally are unable to cause our emotional temperature to return to normal before we must involve ourselves in another situation. It is very hard, therefore, not to let emotions from past situations influence our attitude and our behavior in ensuing situations.

If we have had one hell of a bad day at work, it is very, very difficult, when we get home, to treat our spouse and our children as might be best for them. We often treat them as our emotions dictate rather than as their needs require. Thus, it can be said that we very often carry around some of our emotional hold-overs long after the triggering event has passed.

For example, we were at lunch the other day when a group of friends came in. They spoke and were seated, but they made no move to include my wife and me in their group. To be sure, they no doubt were together by pre-arrangement, but I felt that since we were all friends, they could have invited us to join them. This was a triggering event in my life that I still think about and have hold-over feelings about!

If we are not extremely careful, these emotional hold-overs can cause us to behave in hurtful ways toward others long after the event itself is past.

It is very difficult, after we have been negatively impacted by a number of stress-laden triggering events, for us to be able to have thoughts, judgments, and behavior that is not tainted by our strong emotions.

● **Sources of Our Emotions**
An interesting feature about our emotions, whether they are positive or negative, is that they are not the product of our involuntary response

system. They are the result of the here-and-now decisions that we make, or they are the result of decisions that we have made enough times in the past about similar situations so they have become our habitual way of feeling and reacting. We don't think. We just react!

Our emotions arise from three main sources. The first I have mentioned and is what I call our *habitual emotional responses.* These responses are ways that we learned as children to cope with and to respond to various situations and people. Since they are a habit, we keep right on being "that way."

The sad fact is that many of these emotional response habits that we learned as children may be inappropriate for us as adults. I have an 85-year-old friend whose usual emotional response to social slights and bruises is that of a grade-school girl. She has not updated her emotional responses to be congruent with herself as an adult!

We must be aware of the fact that the important others in our lives may be the captive of their childhood emotional habits. Our challenge, therefore, is to do our job and handle our relationships in ways that will not trigger those negative emotional response habits in others. We must learn to keep our lines of communication open and visible and try to spark in people only positive emotions of trust, security, pleasure and confidence in us.

The second source of our emotions is our own *unique ways in which we see and experience ourselves.* It is part of our concept of our own worthiness, self-esteem, ego, self-confidence, etc. Some situations will spark emotions that seem to be a part of us and are a part of us since they result from how we see and experience ourselves.

I have felt myself to be a very shy person for much of my life. Feeling shy, I behaved in shy ways. I thought that this was my only option, "because I am shy"! Then I learned that my feelings about some situation, person or encounter could be, if I wished, the result of my own decisions.

The third source of our emotions is our own *decision-making process.* "How should I feel?" flows from a triggering event of some kind. Then, "How should I take what he said? Or what he did?" We decide how to feel. Even now as I write this, I am struggling with my childhood emotional habit of feeling slighted, hurt, and angry at not being invited to a friend's party. Yes—the friend owes me one! So, shall I feel slighted and angry? What will it do for me if I do? Will I try to retaliate in some way? It is quite okay for us to go through this kind of self-talk process, for if we do, chances are that our common sense will take over and we will elect not to let the incident make us angry. We can counteract our habitual emotional response system.

When our boss does things that might make us angry, we can elect not to become angry! We must actively re-examine all of our emotional habits to make sure that they are valid.

The fourth source of our feelings emanates from our "*self-talk.*" Sometimes we talk ourselves into having very bad feelings about our spouse, the boss and/or the job. We can make ourselves feel so bad, in fact, that we become demoralized and demotivated. This can be devastating to us and our effectiveness as well as to our relationships. If we are not careful with our self-talk, we will unload all of the blame onto others. We will have become victimized by our own self-delusions!

● **Provide Emotional Safety Valves**

The truths discussed above are among the most powerful forces in the human world. They are at the heart of man's behavior, good or bad, positive or negative, productive or destructive. To my knowledge, however, no one has figured out how we human beings can control our emotions and program our behavior so that we are always positive, always helpful, and always need-fulfilling to others. We just don't program that easily! Nor has anyone, to my knowledge, yet figured out how to always, in all situations, avoid the buildup of the powerful emotional imperatives within us. But we can do some things that will help us in both areas.

The most important thing that we can do is to structure a climate for our group (one-on-one or a larger team) that helps the members of the group to develop together a sense of mutual trust, of mutual concern, and of mutual support; for it is only in such a climate that the members can dare to reveal to others the deep-seated needs and emotions that bug them, beset them, and drive them. It is only with such a group that we can learn to share the depth and force of the emotional imperatives with which we struggle and hope to contain day after day; and it is only through the trusting, sharing, talking, listening, caring process that we can come to terms with ourselves, and in turn, learn to help and to support others with their own similar needs.

● **Conclusion**

One of the most significant things that a boss can do for his subordinates (or that one person can do for another) is to provide them with a safe place to vent their emotions and to talk about their needs—an emotional safe-haven! For it is only through our safely venting our feelings that we can regain and sustain our rational equilibrium.

This kind of climate—this emotional safe-haven—will not automatically develop over time nor emerge at any time without calculated effort. It is a climate that first must be wanted and then be deliberately defined and nurtured by the people involved.

Bill Crockett

● **Discussion Questions**

1. Do you have some negative "triggering events" that are repetitive, i.e., things that happen or that others say or do that "set you off"?
   - If so, what are they?
   - When do they occur?
   - What do you feel when they occur?
   - What are some ways that you might avoid them? List.
   - What might be the consequence of such a discussion?
   - With whom could you discuss these events and your ensuing feelings?

2. Have you ever experienced (been the victim of) someone's emotional imperative in action?
   - How did you feel?
   - How did you react?
   - What was the outcome?

3. Have you ever indulged behaviorally in your own emotional imperative?
   - What was the outcome?

4. As you think about yourself, do you have any habitual emotional reactions that you have carried over from childhood?
   - If so, when do they occur?
   - Have you ever tried to change them?
   - What do they do for you?

5. Have you ever been the victim of someone's act of revenge? Were you aware of what you had done to cause it? How did it turn out? Please discuss.

6. Do you harbor some deeply-held resentments/hurt/anger against someone?

7. Who are some people that you might be able to enlist to join a mutual support group where all of you could talk about "triggering events" in your lives and your ensuing feelings? (You can start with one other person, but three is better.)
   - What is the risk of such a group?
   - How might you raise the subject?

8. Are there ways that you think about yourself that cause you to have negative feelings? If so,
   - How do you handle these?

NOTE: All of these are things that can be shared and discussed with your support group (#7 above) if you will develop one.

THE HUMAN RELATIONS LETTER

Dedicated to the Art of Creating Effective Relationships

Issue #7

OUR EXPECTATIONS—ONE SOURCE OF OUR DISCONTENT

● **Introduction**

Webster defines an expectation as being an anticipated outcome of a relationship or situation. Our expectations can be either positive or negative, depending upon our previous experience. We create expectations about every person and situation that we confront. Our expectations may be based on hard-data; they may be predicated on memories of the way that things once were; or they may have no more basis than the our own wishful thinking—our phantasy of what we hope the encounter might be. Although expectations that have not been explicitly stated are soft data of our own making. we are disappointed when even our wildest expectations are not met. Thus, we produce our own disappointments and create our own discontent.

● **Kinds of Expectations**

There are two kinds of expectations that we each hold of others and which we create in others:

1. Explicit expectations—things that we have said that will or will not be done (promises in the eyes of others), or things that others have said to us that will or will not be done (promises in our eyes).

When anyone tells you that certain things will happen in a certain period, you then have an explicit expectation that these things will occur. When an advertiser promises products, services, and prices, we have a right to anticipate that these things will be forthcoming. When, for whatever reason, these kinds of promises are not kept, we have a right to become upset and angry. We have been mislead, hoodwinked, and deceived.

2. Implied expectations—things that we cause others to believe and that others cause us to believe by the traditions of the past, by implication, by behavior, by hints, by assumptions, etc. In these cases, each person in the relationship carries with him/her a set of expectations that are uniquely related to the relationship and to the situation.

For example, there are implied expectations that go with every role that people assume or relate to in every situation and walk of life—parent, husband, wife, boss, subordinate, child, friend, guest, and hundreds upon hundreds of others. But the most important source of our expectations comes from within ourselves as a result of the data that we have or think we have.

The relationship between a boss and a subordinate provides a fertile field for the planting of implied expectations. The subordinate may do things that the boss doesn't want done, and may not do things that he does want done.

When I was a young man, I was a teller in a small bank. It was my first real job. I was eager, quick, and callow. There were two other tellers in the bank, a man and a woman, both older and more experienced than I. I was a good teller, I thought. I was friendly with people; I handled their business with dispatch; and I got them on their way quickly. People liked to come to my window, and I waited on more than the other two tellers combined. In doing so, however, I postponed doing the things that were a part of each transaction (verifying the totals by adding the checks, sorting and putting away the cash, sorting the checks into proper categories, etc.). By closing time on busy days, my station was a colossal mess—checks unsorted, cash not taken care of, etc. It often took me hours after the other two tellers had balanced and gone home for me to get my work done. And, as one would expect, I hardly ever balanced my books to the penny. I would be over sometimes and short sometimes, but hardly ever could I balance my day's work. I discounted this fact. "Look at those satisfied customers that come to my window," I told myself. My expectation was that my boss would surely reward me for all that I was doing.

One day the boss called me into his office and closed the door. "Here comes the commendation and the raise," I said to myself. You can imagine my shock and my hurt when he said instead, "Bill, I am very concerned about the way that you are doing your job. I get the impression that you are competing with the other two tellers to get the most customers. If this is your intention, you are indeed getting long lines of people at your station. But that is not what I expect of a teller. The cardinal rule of banking is accuracy—balancing the books every night. That is my highest expectation of a teller. And I must say, as you well know, that you have been doing a miserable job on that score."

I had totally misjudged the expectations my boss held for me. Had he been a different kind of man, he might have fired me.

In the case of husbands and wives, either person may not behave as the other expects. The granddaughter of friends was recently divorced.

Why? Because each partner held such different expectations for the marriage that reconciliation was not possible—she wanted children, he didn't! Her implied expectation (not checked out) was that children go with marriage. His expectation (not checked out) was that a career woman wouldn't want children.

Important expectations that are not disclosed at the beginning of a relationship can cause real problems as time goes on.

- **Expectations Often Remain Hidden Data**

The expectations that one person holds for another, as in the cases above, are often hidden. If they are not shared data, neither person is aware of what the other is actually anticipating from the relationship or the occasion. Neither shares.

This is very often the case when a new boss comes on the scene, or when a new spouse enters a family, or when a new subordinate comes aboard, or when two people marry, or when a family plans a trip—or whenever two or more people have any kind of mutual relationship or activity. In most of these cases, each person carries in his/her head expectations (for the other or for the situation) that are based on social norms, experience, hearsay, romantic phantasy, assumptions, etc. And as long as they remain hidden, there really is no way for the other person to fulfill them even if he wants to, except perhaps by chance.

- **Our Disappointment When Our Expectations Are Not Met**

Since we produce our own expectations and often don't share them, we will often be disappointed with the conduct of another who fails our secret test—"Will he/she do the things that I expect of him/ her?"

One of our soft-data creations is our feeling of disappointment when some person's behavior does not measure up to our expectations. This emotional letdown seems to be a very human and natural phenomenon, but it is of our own making. There is no real way in our free society for one person to cause another to behave in ways that will fulfill his self-created expectations. Therefore, when expectations are not made explicit, it would seem only logical for us to be prepared for even our most reasonable expectations to be unmet occasionally.

We can see all about us the harsh and hurtful consequences for people who have had their expectations dashed. It is of no help or consolation to them that their expectations may have been far too high to be realistic in the first place. When the expectations we hold for any situation or for a relationship are finally found to be empty—then bitterness, anger, hostility, and disillusionment are the inevitable results.

It seems to be a truism of life that the more we put our welfare, our future, our happiness into the hands of another—the more dependent we become upon another— the more rage we will experience when we discover that the other has let us down. Divorce, runaway children, and social upheaval are some of the inevitable results of high expectations that have not been fulfilled because no effort was made for the people concerned to get their hidden expectations into the open.

Sometimes, especially in long-standing relationships, although we know by experience and observation what the expectations of the people who are important to us (spouse, boss, parent, etc.) really are, we may risk not fulfilling them!

Many years ago my wife and I lived in Menlo Park, California, and would occasionally drive up to Tahoe for the weekend. One weekend we took guests. We had a pleasant drive up on Friday, a good dinner that evening, and a leisurely day on Saturday. Come Sunday, I was ready to get home to my easy chair and favorite Sunday night TV program. It seemed that others felt the same, so we left Tahoe late in the afternoon. I was driving, and all the others went to sleep.

I knew that my wife expected to stop at a glorified hamburger joint on the way home for a supper of hamburgers, pie, and ice cream. But such a stop would kill at least two hours, and I would miss my programs. So, since everybody was asleep when "The Ground Cow" came into view, I looked the other way and sped on by.

Miles down the road they all woke up.

Wife: "Where are we?"
Me: "Oh, we have just passed Sacramento."
Wife: "Sacramento? You have passed The Ground Cow!"
Me: "Oh yes, miles back."
Wife: "You knew that I wanted to stop there for supper!"
Me: (with feigned innocence) "Oh? Nothing was said about stopping."
Wife: (with more heat) "You know I always want to stop there. If you loved me—!" and so on and so on and so on!

Result? We stopped at another place which was twice as expensive, and it took almost twice as long to get served. And my wife didn't really get over her anger for a week!

Lesson? —When we don't make our expectations *overtly* known to others, they always have the out—"I didn't know!"—even though they could/should have known!

When we let people assume or believe that we will do certain things, we create expectations; then, if we don't fulfill them, the inevitable results are harsh negative emotions—hurt, anger, and bitter

disappointment.
   "If you loved me, you would have known—"
   "If you cared, you would have known—"
   "You should have known—"
are all poignant but stupid and ineffective declarations that get us
nowhere.
   One of the surest ways for us to get into trouble is to *assume* that we
know the expectations of others from the "nonverbal signals" that the
other person gives off or that seem to be built into the situation. Do not
assume under any circumstances that you know the expectations of
another or that another knows your expectations!
   The only sure way of making expectations known is to verbally
state them at the onset of a situation or a relationship.

● **Sharing Expectations**
   The very first thing we need to get into the open with others is our
mutual expectations, both long term and short term. The more important
the relationship is to us, the more important it is for us to get our
expectations shared as early as possible.
   A friend of mine with four young sons planned a family trip from
his home in Northern California to Disneyland. I had discussed the
merits of getting expectations out into the open, so he tried doing it with
his kids, ages six through twelve.
   Father: "Let's make a list of our expectations for the trip. What is
your first one?"
   Kids: "That we will fly to Disneyland, stay in a nice hotel and
spend two or three days at the park."
   Father: "My expectation is that we will all go in the station wagon.
We really can't afford to fly. What is wrong with going by car?"
   Kids: "We know you, Dad. You will fill the tank with gas, Mom
will pack a lunch, and no matter how bad we have 'to go,' you won't
stop until the tank is almost empty. And we don't like to travel like that.
It's no fun!"
   Father: "Well, we can't fly, but maybe we can make the car ride
more fun. Mom will pack a lunch. But when two of you 'have to go,'
I promise I will stop. Would that help?"
   Kids: (looking at each other knowingly) "Oh yes, but we don't
want to eat in the car."
   Father: "When it comes time for lunch, we'll stop at a shady spot
to have a picnic lunch. We'll take a ball and bat, and we'll spend an hour
or so getting the travel kinks out of our legs."
   Kids: "Oh that is great! With those two rules, it will be okay for

us to take the car."

Each different expectation held by the kids and the parents was disclosed, discussed, and accommodation found.

The father told me about this later and said: "It was one of the most pleasant and memorable trips we have ever taken together."

So, take the time to share your expectations and then to make compromises (accommodations) so that the end decision is a win/win for all.

● **Expectations That We Hold for Ourselves**

In addition to explicit and implied expectations, there is another category—the expectations that we hold about ourselves.

We have expectations as to how we will act, what we will do, what we will say, how we will perform in various situations of which are are or will be a part, etc.

In many cases our expectations of ourselves are far too lofty and idealistic for us ever to be able to live up to them, try as we might. Often we lack the self-discipline or the talent or the personality to attain them. As a result, we feel angry, disappointed, and upset because of our failure to fulfill the expectations that we hold for ourselves.

Generally the expectations that we hold for ourselves are kept well hidden from others, especially those who may be closest to us. Then, when these persons don't seem to notice something that we have done or if they react negatively, we feel hurt and even angry with them. Such false expectations can become a perpetual source of irritation and may actually endanger the relationship.

These kinds of expectations are hard to get at and to change because none of us can easily or willingly abandon some of the things that we think we are capable of doing or becoming. This may be where we need to seek professional help.

● **Conclusion**

If we'll tell people about our expectations and discuss their implications, many times people not only can meet them but will also try hard to accommodate us by fulfilling them.

If we'll openly share our expectations with others in advance, then others can tell us the ones that they can't meet, and their reasons, and we can do the same. We can then make compromises and change our plans if necessary so that we won't be surprised and disappointed in the end, and each will know what he/she will receive and give.

Ofttimes people can—should—unhook from unrealistic expectations of others early in a relationship without creating deep emotional reactions when they realize why the other can't fulfill them. By sharing our mutually-held expectations, we can greatly reduce one source of our discontent.

My expectations are that you will read this and will at least give it a try!

Best of luck.

Bill Crockett

● **Discussion Topics**

1. Will you each think of an occasion, situation, or relationship that went sour because expectations were not shared, discussed and accommodated early on? Please describe the situation and what happened. Do you think, had the expectations been discussed in advance, that the outcome would have been different? Why? Why not? Please discuss.

2. Please discuss —Why is it so difficult for people to get their real, deeply-held expectations out into the open? Is it risky? Why do you feel this way?

3. Is the fear of our getting rejected by another when our expectations are discussed early in the relationship more or less hurtful than finding out much later that our expectations (which we haven't disclosed) never had a chance in the first place? What is your experience? Please share an example.

4. Have you had an experience where bosses and subordinates really shared their expectations of each other? How did it come about? How was it done? What were the results? Please discuss.

5. Do you find that the expectations that you hold for yourself are or are not often fulfilled? Could you talk about this with someone that you trust? If not, why not? Please think about what this may be doing to you.

6. Some ways for getting expectations shared are as follows:

● *First way: "My expectations of you are—"* (What you will and won't do for me.)

A. Each person in the group makes a list of his/her expectations of each of the others based on the statement, "I expect that you will **do these things, act in these ways, help with these activities, etc.,** as a result of our relationship."

B. Take turns reading *one* item from each person's list and discuss it. Can you (to whom it is directed) fulfill that expectation? If so, say so! If not, say so and tell why. Then discuss alternatives, reasons, when you might, etc.

C. Continue until all are shared and discussed.

D. Each person then summarize the results of the discussion as it relates to him/her. What is expected of me and what I will do. What I expect of the other and what he/she will do.

E. *Warning*

• Do not agree to an expectation that another holds for you unless you can and will fulfill it and really want the relationship to prosper!

• Don't get angry with the process or with the data surfaced.

• Keep a record.

• Go slowly.

• Don't make false promises.

• Ask questions.

• Listen for understanding.

• Try to accommodate the other!

• It is fair to ask—"Why do you hold such an expectation of me?"

• Follow through and follow up.

F. Talk occasionally to update the lists and tell how things are going.

• *Second way: "I think your expectations of me are—."*

A. Each person in the group makes a list based on the statement, "I think that you expect me to **do these things, act in these ways, help with these activities,** etc. etc., as a result of our relationship."

B. Take turns reading one item from a person's list and discussing it before moving on to another person. If the same expectation is held by another, it should be surfaced at this time. Discuss—Is this really what you think that I expect of you? If you actually have such an expectation, then say so and tell why and how you want it to be. If not, say so and tell why not.

Important Note: It is fair to ask, "How do you come to think that I hold such an expectation of you? What have I done or said that has caused you to make this assumption?" This may give you important data about the implied expectations that you are unwittingly creating by what you are doing or saying. For example, if you are the boss and stay late at night or work on Saturdays when the office is closed, your subordinates may infer that you expect them to do the same. But if you don't expect that—then tell people why you do it!

Important Note: Item #6 above is an excellent process for a boss to use with his/her subordinates (also husband and wife, parents and children). It serves to get a lot of useful hidden data into the open so that it can be dealt with directly.

As a facilitator, I have conducted dozens of such meetings with the end result being uniformly positive. Try it—you might like it—and it really can't make the current situation any worse!

Important Note: Even children four or five years old can play the game of "expectations"!

THE HUMAN RELATIONS LETTER
Dedicated to the Art of Creating Effective Relationships

Issue #8

PROCESS
The Most Fundamental Human Skill

● **Introduction**

Process is the way something—anything—gets done. Process is means. Process is how. Process is well-respected and faithfully used in the hard-data world of science, engineering, mechanics, production, etc. But process is often completely overlooked in the soft-data world of human relationships.

Since the most potent form of process in the human (soft-data) world is behavior, and since we can control/design our behavior, I choose to call process a skill. We can indeed find and use effective processes.

● **Content and Process**

In all human interactions there are two major ingredients—content and process. The first deals with the subject matter or the task upon which the group is working. In most interactions, the focus of attention of all persons is on the content. Substance and working substantive issues require facts, data, and rational ways of thinking, analyzing, and deciding. They are amenable to intellectual attack.

Process, on the other hand, is emotional and behavioral. The way we act—the ways we look, the tone of our voice, and our nonverbal cues—is our process. The way we work and what we do when we work with others is our process. The way I work and what I do when I work an issue with another is impacted both by my attachment to my set of issues (beliefs and perceptions about them), and by the way I experience your behavior toward me and around my issues and my attitudes toward your issues.

Group process, or dynamics, deals with such items as morale, feeling-tone, atmosphere, influence, participation, styles of influence, leadership struggles, conflict, competition, cooperation, etc. In most interactions, very little attention is paid to process, even when it is the major cause of ineffective group action. Sensitivity to group process will better enable one to diagnose group problems early and deal with them more effectively. Since these processes are present in all groups, awareness of them will enhance a person's worth to a group and enable him to be a more effective group participant.

● Some Process Facts

1. There are two parts of every human and group transaction, i.e., the "what," which is the substance, and the "how," which is the process. Substance is our thoughts in action, while process is our emotional reaction to the decisions and to the behavior of the people in the group.

2. The results/product/outcome of every human transaction is the function of task and process—of group members' task skills interacting with their process skills or vice versa.

3. Process in groups can be identified, described and even measured, but it is invisible to the members of the group until they seek to find out about it.

4. There is an optimum process for every situation.

5. The more critical the outcome of a human transaction is to a person, the more care he/she should take in determining what the optimum process should be.

6. No decision should be finally made on an issue until the process for carrying it into action is discussed and decided on.

7. Process has a heavy impact, positive or negative, on the emotions of the people who are involved.

8. Human relationships, therefore, often go asunder, not because of the bad substance, but because of the poor process, i.e., "It wasn't so much what he did as it was the way that he did it!"

9. Good processes in group situations help people to get their four basic needs fulfilled. When good group processes are used, everyone will end up feeling that their needs for power, for inclusion, for security, and for self-esteem have been met!

10. There are really four kinds of soft-data process:

• processes for groups to use in making decisions, interacting and in getting their tasks done— *how.*

• the processes that two people use when they interact together;

• the personal process that we individually use to talk to ourselves as we take in data, interpret it and decide upon action.

• then there is our behavior—the things that we do and say in our interactions with others .. Our behavior is uniquely our own personal process with others, whether we are aware of what we are doing or not.

11. Process need not be—in fact often should not be—an instantaneous reaction to a situation or to another person. The best process may occur after careful deliberation and analysis.

12. Sometimes our process (behavior) is entirely emotionally defensive and reactive. When we permit this to occur, we may be denying ourselves the chance to select the optimum process for the situation.

13. In strictly human terms, we may become more emotionally impacted (upset, angry, demotivated, etc.) by the process and what we infer its meaning to be than we are about the substance itself. "It's not so much what you did that bothered me ('I can see your problem and I even agree with your decision"), but the way that you did it really hurt." And when we experience another's process to be hurtful, threatening, angry, etc., we may become less interested in getting a good product than we are in getting even—somehow!

● **Effective Process**

Process—how we do something for, with and to people—when done effectively is a powerful satisfier of human needs. But ineffective process is a potent dissatisfier, i.e., "it wasn't so much that the decision was bad, it was the way that they did it that got my goat!" etc.

Effective process fulfills people's needs for
    — security
    — belonging
    — influence
    — self-esteem.

Effective process creates the flow of positive emotions in others—security, confidence, trust, honesty, etc.

Effective process helps to lift the fog (the invisible) and helps to make things visible so that they can be dealt with.

Effective process makes people believe that others really do care about them because of the positive meanings they take from the ways things are done.

Effective process sets a tone of trust, support, and openness that eliminates fear and enhances honest discussion

● **Process Is Management Style**

The ways that managers and supervisors elect to do their jobs, the ways they deal with people—their tone of voice and its inflection, the implied meanings of their behavior, the ways decisions are made, the ways meetings are conducted, the ways work is assigned, the ways questions are asked and answered, etc.—is process. Because this process is seen and evaluated by subordinates, it either becomes a powerful force in fulfilling people's needs or in depriving people's needs. The most powerful force in the work environment is that of the perceived meanings of the behavior of the boss, i.e. his process!

The feelings generated by two different "styles" of management (processes) create entirely different feelings in people:

Feelings Generated by the Participatory Process	Feelings Generated by the Authoritarian Process
Positive Emotions	Negative Emotions
Appreciation	Anger, Resentment
Excitement	Boredom
Trust	Suspicion
Loyalty	Alienation
Commitment	Indifference
Interest	Apathy

● **The Key Question for a Manager to Ask Himself**

Before a manager takes an action such as holding a meeting, making a decision, seeing a subordinate, etc.—he should first think about one key question, i.e.,

How do I want the other person(s) to feel when this is all over?

–More secure?	–Less secure?
–A heightened sense of belonging?	–Further alienation?
–A heightened sense of power?	–More impotent?
–More self-esteem?	–More self-doubt?
–Happy?	–Angry?
–More loyal?	–Less Loyal?
–More open?	–Less open?
–More motivated?	–Less Motivated?

Then the manager can list 4-6 processes—things to do and say— that will help to produce the desired emotional state in the other person(s).

The wise manager should then check his decision with a trusted other, i.e., "John, when I hold the meeting to _____, if I do it this way (1),(2),(3),and say these things (1),(2),(3), and use this tone of voice (1), (2), and tell them this (1), (2), (3), will, in your opinion, they feel

(more) (less) secure?
(more) (less) included?
(more) (less) powerful?
(better) (worse) self-image?

Discuss.

If your friend honestly corroborates your own view, then you may have hit upon an effective process to get the job done and leave people feeling like you want them to feel!

● **Process Is an Important Concept for Subordinates to Understand**
The world of process is very important to us subordinates because of our close relationship with two powerful groups, i.e., our boss and our clients. Process for us means that if we have a delicate issue to discuss or to take up with either of these two, we will think through how we will do it before we do anything! What are our options? What are the risks of each? Which, if followed, will best serve our objectives?

It is critical to our success as subordinates that we learn to do this kind of a process- evaluation for each critical issue that we must face!

● **The Most Essential "Hows" (Processes) for Team Members to Know**
Every effective group will take time to discuss their process after the fact. How well did we do this task? There is no end to the processes that relate to people and their relationships. Some of these are—

1. Relationship Processes
2. Meeting Processes
3. Data-Gathering Processes
4. Decision-Making Processes
5. Data-Giving Processes
6. Conflict-Resolution Processes
7. Goal-Setting Processes
8. Action-Planning Processes
9. Status Review Processes
10. Counseling and Coaching Processes
    (Giving and Receiving Feedback)
11. Hiring Processes
12. Orientation Processes
13. Firing Processes
14. Evaluation-of-Work Processes
15. Priority-Setting Processes
16. Confrontation Processes
17. How to Bring About Change Processes
18. Etc., etc.

For example, some of the specific items that a team or family could address and discuss under #1 above are such things as:
• Making Expectations Known
• Making Reasons and Motives Known
• Making Feelings Known
• Making Needs Known
• Having a Defined Goal/Purpose

•Making a Behavioral Contract
•Acceptance of Differences
•Confronting Conflict
•Understanding the Nature of Process
•Understanding the Nature of Hard and Soft
Data
•Wanting to Be/Become Effective
•Willing to Look at Self
•Using the Critique
•Etc.

There is a best way—an optimum process (skill)—for getting each of these things done. Subsequent letters will deal with some of these.

● **Practice Effective Group Processes**
The team should learn to practice effective group processes. Some of these are:

1. Each member should overtly practice being verbally and nonverbally responsive to every issue (suggestion, idea, response, question, etc.) raised by every other member, and most especially by the boss. This means expressing himself/herself! An effective group will not allow an issue to hang, "slowly twisting"! If the issues are no good, the effective group will kill them; if they are good, the effective group will nurture them.

2. Help each other! Listen, respond, support, ask questions for understanding. Give compliments!

3. "Play volleyball" in your discussion of a topic (vs. golf). Bridge your statements and build upon what was said before. Give your motives, reasons and perceptions for what you are about to do. In driving, you use your turn signals; do the same for your conversation! Let people know your intentions!

4. In raising issues and concerns, don't tie them to a suggested solution. Hold the solution until solution time.

5. In finding solutions, first develop as many relevant criteria as possible that the solution must meet. Then measure suggested solutions by the criteria. Don't argue!

6. Keep a list of issues raised which haven't been solved. Prioritize them and hold meetings to solve these saved-up issues. Sometimes the best solution is to throw them out ("We can't solve them!") and then proceed.

7. If you don't understand something, ask! (Especially if you don't understand what's happening *right now*!)

8. Make sure that an issue for discussion or decision is well-defined by the group and that there is agreement on the definition.

9. When disagreeing, practice not being disagreeable. Do not call people names, make insidious comparisons, or behave angrily. If you are angry, then stop the meeting and tell people that you are angry and why.

10. Take responsibility for making the meetings better . Don't leave it all up to the boss.

Each of you knows what's happening to you and what you need at the moment. So take the responsibility for:

—gate-keeping. If the discussion is wandering off, get it back.

—summarizing. If the discussion is starting all over, maybe summarize what has been said and decided, and ask if more discussion is really needed.

—closing. If the discussion ends and there seems to be no closure, tell the group what you heard and ask if that indeed is the consensus-closure.

—helping others get in. If someone is strangely silent, hasn't had a chance to "get in," help that person in by the appropriate words.

—harmonizing. When something is needed by the group—an idea, some words, a reaction, a change of direction—take the risk to initiate something that will help the group.

—asking. When things are really unclear to you, ask!

11. Make sure there is good closure on every issue. This, in effect, means disposing of the issue so that everyone knows what happened to it, i.e., who what, where, why, and when!

12. Observe your process. Occasionally, when things are going extremely well or extremely badly, stop and ask yourself, "What's happening right now? What are we doing? Do we like what we are doing? How should we change it?" And then go on.

13. Bring closure to the meeting by indicating (summarizing) what has been decided for sure; things left open for future discussions (what, when, where, who); things not addressed that will be handled later (what, who, when); other.

14. See that the group does a critique occasionally in order to learn from their own data.

15. Don't argue over hard data. Get the facts.

16. Don't argue around soft-data issues. Practice active listening and using the criteria (#5).

17. Use a "process observer."

The observer's function is only to look at—watch—the *ways* that things are being done, both effective and ineffective, and at stated intervals (every 15 minutes) give a report of what he/she has observed. It is a way of helping people improve their behavior—their effectiveness. It is like the role of a referee in sports who observes the relationship-behavior of the players, not their substance. The process observer seeks to discover whether the behavior of the participants is having a positive or negative impact and then shares it with the group. Who fools whom? Who was off-side? Who blocked well? etc!

● **Conclusion**
Since people are such an unstable medium to work with, the processes that come out well for us today may not work at all the next time we need them (and vice versa). So we must guard against our propensity to decide that we know for sure how to do anything just because it once worked well. Process is a living thing that must be tested and redesigned for each new situation of which we are a part. But—we can—we must learn from the past!
Good luck!

• **Discussion Questions**
1. Do you agree with the process facts stated above? Why? Why not? Please discuss.
2. Please share your own experiences with process which tend to validate one or more of these facts.
3. From your experience, list 3-5 things that people do in groups which are examples of poor process. Please share an experience where people were confronted about their poor processes. What happened?
4. Is lack of awareness of process a problem in your organization? Why? Why not? Discuss.
5. State the problem for managers that the concept of process imposes upon them.
6. How can the modern manager cope with this issue? Discuss.
7. How can the manager or the family bring the invisible process elements into visibility so that they can be dealt with? List. Discuss.
8. Develop three or four recommendations for action that managers or the family could take in order to take advantage of process.
9. What recommendations would you make to top management concerning this issue?

THE HUMAN RELATIONS LETTER

Dedicated to the Art of Creating Effective Relationships

Issue #9

INCONGRUENT BEHAVIOR
The Root Cause of Failure

- **Introduction**

    Webster defines incongruent behavior as our doing things and saying things that do not fit the occasion or situation. It is doing things that are not appropriate, are not suitable, and are not relevant to what is taking place. It is doing things that divert attention, break concentration and introduce extraneous material into whatever is happening at the moment.

    Incongruent behavior is also doing things in the wrong way or doing things half-heartedly so that the outcomes do not achieve the expected goal or target.

    Incongruent behavior applies to the ways that people handle themselves with others, either one-on-one, or in meetings with several other people. It applies to the way that the individual goes about doing his job. And it applies to the way that a group or team carries on its activities.

    Incongruent behavior is any behavior that is ineffective for doing the task at hand. Incongruent behavior doesn't achieve the hoped-for results.

- **Hard-Data Incongruencies**

    The things that we do wrong in the hard-data world are quite easy to spot. Errors in spelling, errors in math, and errors in the processes we use to get results are things that people can quickly recognize and correct.

    Correct ways for executing most sports activities—golf, baseball, skiing, swimming, etc.—have been developed and are taught to both amateurs and professionals. There is a right way, which is congruent behavior, and there is a wrong way, which is incongruent.

    In the world of work, most jobs have well-defined processes and routines which can be learned and, when followed, produce the desired results. The modern assembly-line worker, the computer operator, and the pilot all follow "behavioral congruency" that is at the heart of doing their jobs properly.   Every hard-data discipline has its base of well-defined congruent behavior.

It is our incongruencies in the hard-data world—sports, science, work, etc.—that cause us to fail. We didn't do the process right. Our behavior was incongruent—ineffective—for what it was that we wanted to achieve.

● **Correcting Hard-Data Incongruencies**

The world seems to be obsessed with correcting ineffective behavior in all of its hard-data realms—from cooking to sports, from business to the military, and from pleasure to work. Millions of people are taking "how to" lessons in all kinds of subjects, and hundreds of "how to" books fill our libraries. Our recent miliary engagement in the Gulf, Desert Storm, was a brilliant success because the behavior of our military was so congruent. They did things right.

Of course all of this interest in perfecting our "how to" skills is as it should be. It is a sign of vitality and pride that people want to achieve excellence in the hard-data worlds of their lives.

● **Our Willingness to Learn in the Hard-Data World**

In order for all of this training to happen, people first must come to the realization that they need more instruction—that they aren't doing the best that they can. It means that people aren't defensive about their hard-data deficiencies and therefore they seek help in order to improve. This willingness of people to recognize their own shortcomings is at the heart of their motivation to realize their potential.

In the learning process itself, people must be willing to take critical feedback without being defensive when they do something wrong. This ability to accept feedback about their behavior without being resentful is essential to the learning process.

There are two other things that characterize the hard-data learning process, i.e.,

(1) people's willingness to practice, practice, practice! This requires time and commitment, but it is essential to achieving improvement.

(2) people's willingness to be coached, to seek and accept help. Our willingness to expose ourselves to others so that they can help us is one of the unique concepts of the hard-data world.

A golf pro told me how the world-champion golfer, Jack Nicklaus, came to him for help. "My game is off. Will you help me spot what it is that I am doing wrong (how I am behaving incongruently)?" There was no embarrassment on the part of Mr. Nicklaus. He needed help and he sought it. He got and accepted the help the pro was able to give, and he went on to win the tournament.

● **Our Soft-Data Incongruencies**
Our behavioral incongruencies in the soft-data world—our world of human relationships— are neither easy to recognize, nor to accept, nor to correct. There are a number of reasons for this.

First of all, the soft-data world of human relationships, unlike the hard-data world, does not have a set of standard, structured processes to go by . The human being, with all of his inconsistencies, sensitivity, and moods, is far too complicated and unstable (unpredictable) a base on which to construct a set of hard, fast, and always accurate behavioral principles and processes. But there are some things that we can/should learn so that we can avoid our most blatant incongruencies.

Second, how people behave with and relate to others seems to be "a part of the person," while the way that they swing a golf club, bat a ball, or play cards is "outside" the person! The reality is that both situations involve *behavior*—people in action—but most people see their relationship behavior as somehow being "the real me," not just something they do or the way they do it.

Third, this being the case, the result is that people often feel defensive and are reluctant to seek and accept help. In all too many cases help in this realm is considered as being criticism or an attack on the person. Help is resented and rejected.

The majority of us fail to recognize or to consider the powerful impact that our behavior has on the important others in our lives. We live in a world where we seem to think that our feelings, our intentions and our motives are so well-known to others that they will overlook our ineffective behavior and know, somehow, that we really care and are concerned about them. It is as if no one heeded the consequences that the battering onslaughts of ineffective behavior have on relationships. It's as though we think that "behavior doesn't matter—it's intentions that count"!

Finally and most important, most of us never think of needing to learn processes (skills) (behavior) that will help to make our family, social, and business relationships more harmonious and more productive. People who spend hundreds of dollars on improving their golf games scoff at the suggestion that they might well give "equal time" to improving their own human skills. Because we are people, we all-too-often assume that we somehow are born with these skills in place. Yet we accept the fact that we must learn to play an instrument or to operate a computer. To me, this attitude is indeed a strange and frustrating phenomenon, especially when every paper in the land shouts, with its headlines, the fact that our behavior toward each other has improved little if at all since the time of Christ.

Behavioral modification in the soft-data world is far more complex than it seems to be in the hard-data world. The fact remains, however, that the ways that we have learned to cope with the soft-data situations of life and relationships are very often not very effective. In reality, they are often woefully ineffective—incongruent! The modern-day divorce rate and the number of battered wives and children give ample proof of our behavioral incompetence.

● **The Cost of Incongruent Behavior**

Incongruent behavior, wherever it occurs, has two important negative impacts.

First, it doesn't get the basic job done, whether that job is a product or a relationship. When a person is ineffective, he fails to achieve the results that have been set forth for the endeavor. So by definition, incongruent behavior leads to failure.

Second, there is often an emotional cost to incongruent behavior due to the implied meanings that it carries to others. When people do their jobs poorly or relate to their important others (boss, spouse, child, parent, client, etc.) in inefficient ways, the recipient of such behavior often has the perception that the other doesn't really care. For, if he did care, wouldn't he try to do better the thing that he is failing at?

I was asked by a client to observe the way that he handled an important meeting with a subordinate who had said that he was planning to quit. He said that the subordinate was an excellent employee whom he didn't want to lose. He wanted feedback on his style.

During the interview, I observed that my client (the boss)
—picked at blemishes on the skin of his hands.
—never looked at the subordinate.
—read and shuffled papers on his desk.
—allowed his secretary to put through a telephone call that obviously was of a personal nature.
—asked questions that were not in the context of what the subor‐ dinate had been discussing.
—interrupted the subordinate frequently to tell him how impor‐ tant he was and how much he appreciated his ideas, etc.

When we came to a stopping point, I asked the boss to write down what messages he wanted the employee to receive from the interview.

I asked the subordinate to write down the messages that he had received from the boss.

The boss' list read:

—I care about _____.

—I need him.

—His ideas are sound and should be carried out.

—He has a great future with us.

—We can ill afford to lose him.

—I really don't know why he wants to leave.

The employee's list read:

—He doesn't listen.

—He doesn't care about me.

—He'll never pick up on my ideas.

—I am wasting my time working here.

Then I had the two exchange lists and discuss how they had misread the messages that the other had sent.

The cost of our incongruence is indeed high in the area of relationships.

● **Why Are We So Complacent About Our Ineffective (Incongruent) Behavior in Our Relationships?**

There are many reasons for our complacency; some of the most obvious are the following:

• We don't explicitly define in our own minds how we want the important others in our lives to feel about us. We don't have an explicit behavioral goal.

• We don't explicitly define and identify in our own minds the kinds of behavior on our part that will create positive feelings in the other, nor do we bother to define and identify the behaviors that will cause the opposite, i.e., ill will. This being the case, we do not have a behavioral objective to achieve. We just act as we feel.

• We tend to be blissfully unaware of what our behavior really is at any given time and how it is affecting the other person.

• We tend to act upon our own internal emotional needs rather than acting to fill the emotional needs of others. This inner orientation on our part motivates a self-centered behavior that is oblivious to others. It is often very ineffective if not destructive to our relationships with others.

● **How Does One Get at the Problem of Incongruent Behavior in the World of Relationships?**

There are six things that two people, or a team, or a family can do in order to surface behavioral incongruencies and work toward improvement. These are:

1.   Develop together the goals that they want to be achieved in the relationship. This includes such things as trust, honesty, caring, support, respect, etc.

2.   Develop together a list of behaviors—things that people will say and do—that will be congruent with each of the goals and make them viable. Then create a list of behaviors which, if followed, will be hurtful to the goals (incongruent behaviors).

3.   Agree that all involved will help each other with monitoring their individual behavior as to its congruency or incongruency around each of the goals, i.e., "When you do _____, you are not congruent with goal _____."

4.   Agree that each will not be defensive, hurt or angry when others give them feedback about their behavior.

5.   Agree that each person will develop a simple action plan for his/her own improvement.

6.   Meet occasionally to summarize what has happened, who has done or not done what, and to get feedback on improvement, etc.

Note: The above is called a "Behavioral Contract." It is especially effective for a work team or a family group.

● **Conclusion**

It is always surprising to me when I consider the vast difference between the huge effort we make to improve our hard-data "how to" behaviors versus the paucity of the efforts we make to improve our ability to relate to others in positive ways. It is very easy to find excuses for this difference, but considering the tremendous importance of achieving and maintaining positive relationships, the excuses are hardly convincing. The only way for us to do better is to start, and there is no better time to start than now! So good luck!

Bill Crockett

● **Questions for Discussion**

1.   Please describe a situation where incongruent behavior caused problems. Discuss the pros and cons.

2.   What are some of the most common relationship incongruities between

—husbands and wives?

—bosses and subordinates?

—parents and children?

Please share and discuss. What needs to be done in each case?

3. (a) Please list a number of your most important relationships. Select one.

(b) Now list the meanings that you want that person to feel about you, like

he cares.

he is considerate.

etc.

(c) Next list the behaviors that you must employ—use—in order for your behavior to carry the meanings.

(d) Now evaluate yourself—your real-life behavior on the list (c).

(e) Do this in pairs, exchange lists and discuss.

(f) How *congruent* is your behavior?

Note: The most effective way of doing this is for the people concerned to do it together.

4. Describe some lessons that you have taken to improve some game that you play.

—What did the instructor do/say?

—How did you respond?

—What have you done since?

—What has been the effect on your game?

Could you do the same thing with some trusted others about your relationship incongruencies? If not, why not? If so, describe, discuss.

Note: With the right climate, this is an excellent team-building exercise.

Important note: It no doubt will require professional help for a person to delve into himself to find the cause, the *why*, of his behavior. And it is certainly inappropriate for us to pretend that we know the *whys* of others' behavior, although we often try. But almost anyone—any important other—can describe the hard-data *what* of your behavior and can divulge the messages that it carried for him. This is not a game of "Let's play doctor." It is real life, i.e., "I want my behavior to tell you _____. If it is not telling you that, then help me to understand."

THE HUMAN RELATIONS LETTER
Dedicated to the Art of Creating Effective Relationships

Issue #10

THE LAW OF RECIPROCAL BEHAVIOR
Source of Evil—Source of Good

"I'LL GET EVEN WITH YOU!"

- **Introduction**

One of the early learnings that we pick up as children is that of reciprocal behavior—"I'll get even with you!" "You started it" is the excuse often given for almost any conflict, including war (a good example is the recent conflict in the Gulf). The earliest documents about human relationships are filled with examples of this human folly. We see this force being acted out in the "horseplay" of siblings—the hitting, the pinching, the running, hiding and yelling. In children it may be an amusing pastime, but in adults it is a tragic form of immature, uncivilized behavior. Unhappily, it is a behavior that is rampant throughout our adult world. We see it exemplified in our defense policy (the retaliatory first strike), in our foreign relations, in our businesses, in our personal relationships, and throughout society as a whole. "Get even" is the conventional wisdom of the day.

But the simple process of "getting even" never ends. It escalates the emotions of both sides so that all kinds of heinous acts are committed, which are then fully justified in the minds of the perpetrators. The deep-seated animosities that fuel the waring factions in Beirut, in North Ireland and elsewhere show how really tragic this behavior is to the people involved. It is an evil business at best. Yet, hardly anyone ever wants to stop it by being the first to "give in."

So on and on it goes, reaping its tragic harvest of ruined lives and relationships.

- **Legitimate Retaliatory Behavior**

When we, in our relationships with our families or others, cause pain and hurt, we can generally expect some form of retaliatory behavior to come back to us! This is understandable and acceptable when what we have done was a deliberate act on our part to hurt and injure the other. We may deserve to be punished.

We also can expect some form of retaliatory behavior from our bosses when we have failed them. We will be reprimanded or even discharged if we don't do our jobs well and fail to meet their expectations! We know the rules of the game. And of course, if we break the law, we can expect to be punished. This also is a rule of the game.

But the person with the power, the manager, must be very careful in the ways that he uses his power. There are reports from management consultants and psychologists that people look to exact revenge when they perceive that they have been unfairly hurt, slighted or damaged by their supervisors. The article, "Sweet Revenge Is Souring the Office," (*Wall Street Journal*, Wednesday, Sept. 19, 1990) is one that carries important lessons for managers. Two books relating to this subject are: *Woman to Woman—From Sabotage to Support* by Judith Briles, and *Confessions of an SOB* by Al Neuharth. These are worth the manager's time.

- **Vengeful Retaliatory Behavior**
Revenge can take many forms. Sometimes the one getting even hides himself from the knowledge of the victim so that the victim is hurt but doesn't really know the source of his pain. But the one who does the hurting knows and is fulfilled by his evil act of retribution. This is often the tactic that the terrorist uses with his victims.

This is also the way a worker on the production line can get even by failing to complete some process such as tightening all of the big bolts, etc. It is the tactic used by cooks in even the fanciest restaurants to get even with crusty, demanding and arrogant customers.

You no doubt have heard the airline story of the mean customer who abused the check-in clerk. When he had gone, the next customer sympathized with the clerk. The clerk said, "Oh, I have already gotten even with him!" "How is that?" "He is going to Chicago, but his baggage is already on its way to Alaska!"

This hurtful, childish give-and-take can infect families, businesses, and even nations. Once started, the process escalates and there often is no way to painlessly end the feud. There are documented cases where disappointed employees, jilted lovers, and frustrated people of all kinds have actually committed cold-blooded murder to get even. The emotions that are aroused in people in these cases are among the most powerful and most frightening that we humans have to deal with. They are motivators of blind behaviors that ignore all moral and legal restraints.

- **Our Challenge**
The powerful nature of this "law" of reciprocal behavior makes it urgently important that we not do things that will cause this law to be applied in negative, hurtful ways by the people who are important to

us—bosses and subordinates—husbands and wives—clients—parents and children. This means that we should be very aware of ourselves, our style of managing, our methods of communicating, and the ways that we come across to others. It is inexcusable for a manager at any level to unwittingly behave in ways that will activate this dreadful chain reaction. It is the responsibility of the modern manager to know how he does come across to people. It is the responsibility of the organization to be aware of the human results (costs) of their management style!

High levels of waste, high rates of attrition, high rates of absenteeism, low productivity, and low morale are all symptoms of this negative force at work.

● **The Good News**

But—there is good news—this law not only works in negative ways, giving hurt for hurt, but it can also work in positive ways — giving favor for favor.

We can use the law of reciprocal behavior to garner positive feelings and powerful support from others by extending favors, by fulfilling the important needs of others, by speaking out in the defense of others, and by making others aware that we do care for them. We can see these positive, loving, win/win relationships in families, in businesses, and in public groups, just as we can see the negatives. It is the positive application of this law which is the basis of our win/win networks.

It is the operation of this law that makes it so important for us subordinates to treat our bosses and our clients well—to cheerfully meet their needs, to fulfill their expectations and make sure that they perceive us favorably.

In one of my favorite restaurants I have a favorite waiter who makes me feel great in the presence of my guests. Whatever change in menu a guest may ask for, his cheerful (not hedged or grudging) response is "no problem!" He meets my needs. As a result, he earns for himself, by this behavior, big tips; and he earns for his boss, the owner, lots of business from me and lots of praise for his restaurant. The law of reciprocal behavior (in the positive) is at work.

It is this kind of reciprocal behavior that puts force and vitality in our win/win networks! It is this kind of behavior that is the bond of friendship. Thus, positive reciprocal behavior is a powerful tool for all of us to learn to use.

The extra bit of work that our subordinates do for us without our asking, the unsolicited words of praise that come to our supervisors from our clients, and the always welcome words of praise that come to us from our bosses, are nothing more nor less than this powerful law in action. It works.

● **Conclusion**

The law of reciprocal behavior, of course, is not really a law in the hard-data sense of the word. But it works; and in its negative application, it works all too often.

What can one do to avoid or to stop the vicious negative cycle? There are three things that we can do, i.e.,

1. First, we can make sure that we behave positively (the things that we do, don't do, say and fail to say) toward the people who have it in their power to hurt us. By so doing, we do not arouse the vindictive urge in them. This means that we behave in civil ways in all circumstances—we don't yell at subordinates, we don't frustrate bosses, we don't insult customers (even the nasty ones), we don't hog the road (in California people get shot for doing this), we don't forget our anniversary, etc. etc.

There is an old saying: "Hell hath no fury like a woman scorned," but we should enlarge it to say: "Hell hath no fury like a person who feels that he has been unjustly (or deliberately) wronged or slighted (hurt)"! So—don't evoke those emotions in others! Restrain yourself!

2. We can monitor our own feeling-state to make sure that we recognize these evil feelings when they come up inside of us and then that we do not act upon them! One must be an extraordinarily good person if he never feels the urge to "get even" (to tell someone off) who has caused him pain, trouble and hurt. But one can, even though he may have some legitimate reason to retaliate, refrain from taking the retaliatory actions! This means that we don't allow ourselves to be pulled into the vicious cycle in the first place—we have controlled ourselves!

3. Once into this retaliatory cycle, we can opt out anytime that we want to do so by not taking the next retaliatory step. It takes two to play the game, so if we at any point refuse to play, then the game ends. The problem is that this is much easier said than done. There is so much emotional release and satisfaction for us in the act of "getting even" that it is hard for us to stop. It is a habit almost as addictive as dope and almost as hard to break. Again, North Ireland, Beirut, the PLO, and South Africa are tragic examples of the never-ending nature of the problem.

The poems which follow give us some additional insights.

Good luck.

Bill Crockett

NEVER LOSE YOUR COOL

When life for you starts going wrong
And bitter words would be your song,
When no one wants to play your game
And no one cares that you're hurt and lame,
When you're pushed around and feel the fool,
Then, take it easy—control yourself—
And never lose your cool!

When you're very mad and really can't wait
To spill all your guts and set them straight,
Then you've lost your own game by what you have done!
Yes—you've lost a game that you might well have won!
The one who burns bridges is really a fool—
So, take it easy—control yourself—
And never lose your cool!

The one who can smile in the fact of fate
And can take what comes without bitterness and hate,
The one who can forgive and not vengeance seek
And can stand against wrong, yet turn the other cheek,
The one who can live by the Goldenn Rule—
He will win in the end!
So take it easy—control yourself
And never lose your cool!

MOTIVES

I see me by my intent
Which is today just fine.
How you can think so ill of me
I really can't divine!

I see you by the ways you act.
Your motives aren't expressed.
But judging by the things you do,
They surely aren't the best!

But if I can tell you why I hurt
And you respond in kind,
Perhaps together we can learn
To neither be so blind!

VENGEANCE IS SWEET

I'll get even with you!
You knew it would hurt!
You wallow in dirt!
But I'll get even with you!

You'll be sorry before we are through,
For this day I shall ever recall.
And I savor the thought most of all
That some day I'll get even with you!

Oh, once we were friends, 'tis true;
But you swept me aside
Like seaweed on the tide,
And for this, I'll get even with you!

And when I do get even with you,
How sweet it will be when I see
Your futile entreaty to me!
Then I'll know that I'm even with you!

• • • • • • • •

● **Questions for Discussion**

1.   Please share an experience where you felt hurt or slighted (work or social).
         —What did the other do?
         —How did you feel?
         —What did you do?
         —What were the outcomes?

2.   Please share an experience where you set out to "get even."
         —What caused the situation?
         —What were your feelings?
         —What did you do?
         —What was the outcome?

3.   Please share an experience where you or another had "good cause" to take retaliatory action but did not do so.

—What was the situation?
—Why wasn't action taken?
—What was the outcome?

4. Please share a situation at work where people got even with the boss or the establishment.
—What was the situation?
—What did people do?
—What was the outcome?

5. Please share an experience where good was returned for evil.
—What was the circumstance?
—What happened?
—What was the outcome?

6. Please share an experience where the evil retaliatory cycle was broken and people settled their differences.
—What was the situation?
—How was it settled?
—Who initiated the first act of settlement and why did (he)(she) do so?
—What was the outcome?

7. Please share an experience where the climate was positive and people cared for and helped each other.
—How did it come about?
—What were the benefits?
—What was the outcome?

8. Sometimes this negative behavior can start to operate in a very minor way at home, at work, or in a social setting. "You don't do 'X' for me so I won't do 'Y' for you!"
    A way to help break the cycle and get the people concerned (family or team) onto a positive track is to do the "behavioral contract" exercise, i.e.,
    a) Each person in the group writes the answers to these statements about *every* other person in the group:
    (1) It helps (helped) me when you (describe some action).
    (2) I appreciate the way you (describe some action).
    (3) It would help me if you would (describe) because I_____(explain) .
    (4) It would help me if you could stop (describe) because I (explain) .

       (5)   Would it help you if I would <u> (describe)</u>?

b) Now, start with one person:

       (1)   Each of the others read their #1 and #2 statements. Go slowly; let the recipient have time to savor the positives.

       (2)   Now each person read his #3 statement. If more than one person has the same request, then the recipient should carefully consider his response.

            Take time—discuss—get agreement.

       (3)   Now go on to #4 and #5.

c) Do this for each person in the group. It may take more than one session.

d) Talk about how each person wants to be told (helped) when he "slips."

e) Talk about the next meeting for a review.

f) Make it fun.

Note: The youngest children can participate in this "game." They won't be able to write their answers, but they will *know* what they would like!

OUR NEEDS
Part A

● **Introduction**

There is a vast difference, in many cases, between what we feel that we need and what we really need. It is the wise person who can discern the difference and then discipline himself to accept the reality.

Webster defines a need as being something that is required by us. And the great conceptual psychologist, Abraham Maslow, added the idea that when our needs are unmet, they become powerful motivators of our behavior.

Dr. Maslow defined a whole hierarchy of both psychological and physiological needs that we all must deal with. For the purposes of this letter, however, we will consider only four powerful psychological needs: security (survival); inclusion (belonging); power (potency); and self-esteem (ego). This letter also departs somewhat from Dr. Maslow's concept of hierarchy and treats all four of these needs as being equally prevalent in modern society.

● **Facts About Our Needs**

It is strange how our needs seem to work.

Like ears and noses, all people have these four fundamental psychological needs. To be sure—a Kurd in a soggy tent in Iraq may have a primary need for physical comforts, but that same person also will feel some deep psychological needs as well, i.e., survival, for example.

Different people can have different needs and different levels of the same needs when they are faced with the very same conditions. Some will react one way and some another. And our own need levels change from time to time, from situation to situation, and as we ourselves change, experience and mature over time. What frightened me yesterday no longer holds any fears for me today.

Maslow held that it is our unmet needs that drive us and motivate us to take the actions that will satisfy those needs and get them back into balance.

Our unfulfilled needs manifest themselves through our emotions—

our feelings. When these feelings are strong, they set up within us what I call an "emotional imperative"—an almost irresistible demand for us to take action that will bring the need back into balance and thus rid us of that pressing imperative to act!

The risks of our immediately fulfilling our emotional imperative with redressing kinds of actions are severe. First of all, the actions that we take are often precipitous—taken hastily without any thought given as to either their appropriateness or to their possible impact upon the receiver. Therefore, while the actions may indeed fulfill our own immediate feelings (needs), they may be quite ineffective for us in the long run because of their negative impact upon our important other who has been the recipient of our rash behavior.

It is also interesting to contemplate how blissfully unaware we are of the existence of the underlying needs that drive our behavior. We just automatically respond to our feelings. We also are oblivious to the negative impact that need-driven behavior has upon the important others in our lives.

The most common kinds of need-driven behavior are such things as defensiveness, denial, perfectionism, workaholism, authoritarianism, addictiveness, aggressiveness, violence, criticism, bad-mouthing, bragging, self-aggrandizement, shyness, self-pity, self-effacement, self-centeredness, depression, and so on—all examples of dysfunctional behavior.

This kind of behavior is so much a part of the person's habitual way of acting that it seems to be (is) an integral part of the person's personality. When confronted about this dysfunctional behavior, the person may simply respond, "That is me." "That is the way I am." etc., as if he/she couldn't possibly change nor see a need to change. Such people remind me of the poem—

ME CHANGE?

Whatever I am, I have come to be
And that's what I like, for that is me.
To ask me to act in a different way
Is like trying to turn the night into day.

I won't feel good—it won't seem right
To make a change, however slight.
Just accept the person whom you see,
For that's who I am. That's the real me!

But—whatever I am, I have learned to be,
So I can learn to change to some degree.
I'll take the risk, 'cause I'm anxious to see
What kind of a person will be the new me.

Another phenomenon about this kind of behavior is that it will become our habitual way of responding to people and to situations over time, so that what we do and say is quite thoughtless and automatic. It just comes out.

● **The Relationship Bind That Needs Can Cause**
Since we all have these needs which call us to action, we may find ourselves in competition with another who is trying hard to get his very same need met. Two people with high ego needs will usurp the air time of everyone in their competition to be heard—to get their own needs met. In a social setting, this may not be of much consequence, but when the two are boss and subordinate, the result may be devastating for the subordinate. This situation is uniquely illustrated by a press story about President Bush and his then Chief of Staff, Governor Sununu. The story tells how the press criticized Mr. Sununu for a statement that the President had made in a recent speech. In frustration and anger, Mr. Sununu flared:
"I did not put that into the President's speech. He ad-libbed it."
Mr. Sununu's need, whatever it was, took priority in his behavior over the best interests of his boss, President Bush. This is a very good way to get one's self fired. (Mr. Sununu subsequently resigned.)
When this same conflict of needs arises in families, it can result in deep personal conflict and animosity.

● **The First Step—Recognize Our Own Needs**
One way for us to recognize what is going on with us is to become aware of our deep-seated feelings and our subsequent behaviors. Of course, if we are lazy, complacent and self-satisfied, what follows is not for us. Only if we wish to become and be truly effective in our relationships, will we take the trouble to examine ourselves. Here are some clues for us to look for.

● **Our Security (Survival) Need**
• This is one of our most primitive and instinctive human needs. This need manifests itself when we
— encounter new people.

— enter new situations.

— change from the tried and true to something new.

— have our territory threatened.

— encounter danger or what we perceive to be danger.

— encounter threats of violence.

— etc.

• Some of the feelings that occur when this need is high are suspicion, fear, and anxiety.

• The behavior that we elect to take in order to cope with this unfulfilled need ranges from total flight (submission) on the one extreme to total aggression (fight) on the other.

We are all so different that it is virtually impossible to generalize about how people will react, even to the same situation, but there are great historical examples of how people have survived the most dreadful conditions over long periods of time simply because this survival need is so powerful in us. The U.S. prisoners who were systematically mistreated in the Hanoi Hilton and the hostages of the Middle East terrorists are but two examples that could be cited. People are indeed tough and have learned to cope.

The way we elect to cope is often the real problem. The coping behavior that comes into play in the situations mentioned above is quite appropriate. But often we respond to situations with our friends, relatives and associates as if we were lost in the jungle's no-man's-land.

● **Our Need for Inclusion—To Be Part of a Group, a Team, a Family**

• This, too, is one of our primitive needs, perhaps stemming from the need to belong to a group in order feel more secure. To feel that one does have an acknowledged place in a group does lead to feelings of more personal security. This need manifests itself when it seems that we are excluded from activities that we should be in, when we're not wanted, and when we are left out.

• Some of the feelings that emerge when this need is deprived are:

— loneliness.

— alienation.

— anger.

— indifference.

— self-doubt.

— suspicion.

— hate.

• The behavior that we elect in order to cope with our unfulfilled belonging need ranges from total obsequiousness on the one hand to harsh, vindictive punishment on the other.We are so different that it is virtually impossible to generalize. But we can generalize that whatever the behavior, it probably won't be very effective in our relationships with others.

We see this behavior manifest itself in businesses where management has distanced itself from the workers and in homes where the parents aren't much involved with their children.

- **Our Need for Power, or Potency**
Another important and basic human need is that of power, or potency. This means our need to have influence over the things and decisions that impact us and of which we are a part. One of the important by-products of permitting people to have influence and inputs into the decisions on matters which they are responsible for implementing is their increased sense of commitment.
  - This need manifests itself when we are not asked our opinion, when we are not included in decisions, when we are told what others decided for us—what we do when, how, where, etc.
  - Some of the feelings that occur in people when this need is not fulfilled are:
    — frustration.
    — anger.
    — hate.
    — self-doubt.
    — vindictiveness.
    — despair.
  - The behavior that people elect in order to cope with their unfulfilled power needs ranges all the way from opting out at one extreme ("What the hell! Who cares?"), thereby assuming no responsibility and feeling no commitment (perhaps even resorting to some subversion in order to cause the decision to fail), to becoming virtual tyrants in areas where they do have the power to control.

- **Our Ego Need**
Finally, there is our ego need, our self-esteem, our self-worth need.
  - This involves our sense of worthwhileness, our sense of well-being, and our sense of being respected by others. To some extent, this need is the culmination of the other three needs having been fulfilled and to the degree they have been or have not been met. This need is often triggered by some early experiences in our lives, the tapes of which seem to make us have opinions about ourselves regardless of the evidence to the contrary.

• This need, when it is deprived, perhaps more than any other must be worked hard in order to come to a healthy appreciation of one's self.

• Some of the feelings that we have when this need is unfulfilled are:

— shyness.
— lack of confidence.
— fear.
— anxiety.
— despondency.

• The behaviors that we use to cope with this need range from almost total self-effacing inaction at one extreme to totally aggressive, egotistical behavior at the other.

— Behavior that people often use to fulfill this need includes self-effacing statements, withdrawal, self-putdowns, excessive egotism, etc.

● **When Our Needs Get Out of Hand**

As I have already said, our needs are a part of our human system. We are stuck with them. Our needs are potentially destructive to us only when we permit them to get out of hand—when we have lost control of ourselves, when we have given in to our addictions, when we don't recognize our own habitually ineffective need-oriented behavior, and most important, when we don't give a damn anyway as to how we are perceived by others. In such cases, we have let our our needs rule our lives to the extent that we have become behaviorally ineffective with our important others.

● **What to Do?**

There are three things for us to do if we suspect that we have fallen into some ineffective need-driven habits, and we do want to become/ be more effective.

First, we must get some hard data about what we ourselves are feeling when the need is triggered. Since our feelings are the manifestation of our needs, we can become aware of our need by becoming aware of our feelings. This is the ah-ha step—"Ah-ha! I have caught you!"

Second, once the feeling and the need are recognized, the task is to pinpoint the situations that have triggered the need in the first place. It is only if we can identify the triggering events and our subsequent feelings can we take remedial action. This puts us on guard against the kinds of things that cause the need to surface. Awareness is the beginning of the cure.

Third, once we know the feeling and are aware that the need has surfaced, we must absolutely refrain from taking the old habitual action! This means putting a leash on the raging monster inside of us that is demanding that we do something, This means stopping our words before they are spoken! It means trying to gain enough personal satisfaction from our restraint to offset the deprived feeling that we have for not taking the action that we normally would have taken.

It means recognizing our feelings but electing not to act on them.

It means taking charge of ourselves.

It means changing ourselves.

● **Conclusion**

I don't know when or how our needs get started. But I do know that our indulgence in satisfying them will often lead to our own pain and even destruction. Most certainly it can lead to alienating our closest friends and most important others, including our boss.

I also know from my own personal experience that we can put our needs under our own personal control if we really want to and if we really care about our own effectiveness as a human being.

But curbing our own needs is but half our responsibility; the other responsibility is in making sure that we do not cause needs to arise in the people who are important to us. Part B of this letter deals with that issue.

But don't diagnose the needs of others. The needs themselves are deeply hidden data. All that we can see in another is the behavior. We can suspect the motive, but we can't really be sure. So don't label people by giving them needs—just deal with their behavior and its impact on you.

Bill Crockett

● **Discussion Topics**

1. In a work team or in a family, it is often worthwhile to do a "needs evaluation exercise." It is done as follows:

    a. Make sure that the people are aware of the four psychological needs and the attendant feelings.

    b. Talk about the fact that when a need is fully satisfied, it is at zero. It is not causing a feeling and therefore it is not pressing us to action—to do something.

    c. Discuss the fact that when a need is not satisfied, it will register itself in our feelings, like having a fever will register itself on a thermometer. So each need is like a thermometer.

OUR NEEDS FOR

Security   Belonging   Power   Ego

100   100   100   100

0   0   0   0

    d. Tell them, "Become aware of your own feelings and try to relate them to one of the four psychological needs. Then mark on the appropriate chart how strongly that need seems to be."

    e. Tell them, "Now try to pinpoint the situation, the person, the behavior, etc., that causes these feelings to arise in you."

    f. Now, discuss each person's rating—the feelings and the behavior that the group sees. Also discuss what both the person himself as well as what others might do that would help to satisfy the needs of each.

    g. Closure and action plans—who will do what and when, and when will we discuss it again.

OUR NEEDS

I am your all-consuming needs.
I own your soul – your mind – your deeds.
You cannot live a life that's free
Until you first have dealt with me!

I cause the way you feel each day.
I impose myself in every way.
You must accept the things you do,
For I often make a fool of you!

I'm more possessive than any dope,
And thus, without me, you cannot cope.
You cannot live a life that's free
Until you first have dealt with me!

Of all addictions great and small,
It's our feeling needs that top them all!
It's up to us to sort them out –
We must take charge! We have the clout!

OUR NEEDS
Part B

- ### Introduction

It was suggested in the conclusion to Part A that one of the things that we can do to be more effective with the important others in our lives is to behave in ways that help people to get their needs met—or to put it another way—behave in ways that do not actually cause people to feel more need-deprived, i.e., more insecure, more lonely, more impotent and less worthwhile. It seems to me that no thinking/caring person would deliberately go about causing such pain in their important others, yet we all do it simply by the ways that we act and talk.

- ### How Can I Know?

The lists that follow are not all inclusive, but if answered honestly, they will give a person an idea of how well he fulfills the needs of his important others. And, if you have someone who will be honest with you, you can ask them to give you their perceptions.

This is an excellent exercise for a boss and his team or for parents with each other and/or with their children. The only going-in stipulations are (1) that people won't become angry or hurt when the others' ratings are low. These must be treated as gifts of great value—pearls from friends who love you enough to be honest with you; and (2) of course there is no point in doing the exercise if one does not plan to change if the data suggests that change is called for. So, action plans must be discussed and decided on.

When important others rate any of the items, high or low, it is a good idea for them to have some specific behavioral examples in mind that illustrate their rating. And don't do all four at one sitting! Do one, work it, work the action plans, and at some later date do another. There is no advantage served by overloading anyone with too much data.

Rate   Have An
Yourself Important
Here   Other Rate
         You Here

0 = hardly at all
10 = very well

HOW WELL DO I HELP OTHERS TO FEEL SECURE?

How well do I —
1. Tell people the reasons for my decisions, plans and viewpoints?
2. Tell people my motives for the things that I do?
3. Tell people my expectations of them in advance?
4. Tell people at the time how well they have fulfilled my expectations?
5. Give people positive feedback for jobs they have done well?
6. Explain to people what's going on with me emotionally so they won't have to wonder and worry that they have "made me......."?
7. Refrain from nitpicking the work/decisions of others?
8. Behave calmly in crisis situations?
9. Refrain from badmouthing others to my peers and subordinates?
10. Retain consistency of reaction, program and purpose?
11. Recognize emerging problems quickly?
12. Make needed decisions without undue delay?
13. Develop well-defined goals, objectives and standards for people?
14. Bring about closure in meetings by summarizing decisions made (what, who and when)?
15. Train people so that they can succeed?
16. Define areas of responsibility and authority so that there is no ambiguity in getting the job done?
17. Do not accept substandard performance without taking remedial action?
18. Listen to people's feelings and concerns?

19. Make sure that people are properly introduced, oriented and made to feel comfortable? ____ ____
20. Support the ideas of others? ____ ____

HOW WELL DO I HELP OTHERS TO FEEL THAT THEY HAVE INFLUENCE?

How well do I —
1. Get people's data, information, and ideas before I make decisions? ____ ____
2. Include people in making the decisions that they must carry out? ____ ____
3. Give freedom to people to do their jobs which I have delegated? ____ ____
4. Share future plans with people? ____ ____
5. Give people latitude on how to do their jobs? ____ ____
6. Involve people in setting standards? ____ ____
7. Involve people in goal-setting? ____ ____
8. Let people represent me in important situations? ____ ____
9. Let people have authority for making important decisions? ____ ____
10. Change my mind when people tell me that I am on the wrong track? ____ ____
11. Accept differing points of view that people hold? ____ ____
12. Give people my support and encouragement? ____ ____
13. Tell people my plans and decisions? ____ ____
14. Support people's decisions? ____ ____
15. Ask and accept the help/advice of people? ____ ____
16. Listen to and acknowledge people when they talk? ____ ____
17. Tell people how well their advice/ideas/suggestions have worked out for me? ____ ____
18. Tell others the good/positive points about people? ____ ____
19. Not take up all the air time when I am involved with others? ____ ____
20. Not publicly disagree or put down the ideas of others? ____ ____

HOW WELL DO I HELP OTHERS TO FEEL INCLUDED?
How well do I —
1. Listen to people without fidgeting, interrupting and doing other things? ____ ____
2. Stay accessible to people? ____ ____

3. Include people in meetings when their personal
and professional interests are at stake? ___ ___
4. Take an interest in people's situations beyond the
job itself? ___ ___
5. Keep people well informed of what's going on in
the organization? ___ ___
6. Talk to people about their feelings about themselves,
their work, their needs, and how I can help them? ___ ___
7. Share with people my own feelings so they can
understand me better? ___ ___
8. Know people's names, interests and jobs? ___ ___
9. Know people's special problems of health, family, ___ ___
etc., that may impact their job performance or their
attitudes? ___ ___
10. Know people's plans and ambitions and help them
achieve them? ___ ___
11. Tell people honestly, directly and caringly their
failures, shortcomings, lack of effectiveness, and how
they can do better? ___ ___
12. Not create a state of dependency in people? ___ ___
13. Support people when they need help? ___ ___
14. Give people credit for what they have done in
carrying out ideas that were not originally mine? ___ ___
15. Help people have air time to express themselves? ___ ___
16. Include people in my personal activities so that they
will know that I care? ___ ___
17. Not talk too glowingly about my activities which
did not include the people present? ___ ___
18. Help people to understand how important they
really are to me? ___ ___
19. Let people help me when they offer? ___ ___
20. Accept the ideas and suggestions of people? ___ ___

HOW WELL DO I HELP OTHERS TO FEEL IMPORTANT (SELF-ESTEEM)?

How well do I —
1. Refrain from criticizing people publicly? ___ ___
2. Refrain from putting people down by voice tone,
gestures and words? ___ ___
3. Refrain from questioning people's motives and
reasons for mistakes—"Why.....?" ___ ___

4. Refrain from over-controlling people's plans, time, methods, etc.? ____ ____
5. Refrain from making people "eat crow" by forcing them to admit being wrong? ____ ____
9. Help people to find things that they can do well and succeed at? ____ ____
10. Observe civility in talking with people? ____ ____
11. Refrain from making people do everything my way? ____ ____
12. Help people to feel good about themselves? ____ ____
13. Listen to people? ____ ____
14. Take the initiative in doing things for people that show that I care? ____ ____
15. Make sure that I acknowledge people's contributions, efforts, and help? ____ ____
16. Help people to have air time to express their ideas, suggestions, differences? ____ ____
17. Stay aware of what is going on in all situations so that I can be of help to people? ____ ____
18. Not act like I am the final authority on all subjects? ____ ____
19. Not second-guess what people have done after the fact? (I told you so!) ____ ____
20. Not make invidious comparisons of people with others? Oh, you should see what X has done!) ____ ____

● **Conclusion**

You have several options with this letter or with any of the other letters of the series. The first option—pitch it—is the one that I hope you don't choose!

The second option—read it—is slightly better than the first. There may be a small benefit from doing only this. "Um-um—interesting. Maybe I'll get around to doing something about it one of these days." And then it is swallowed up in oblivion along with all of our other good intentions.

The third option—share it with a trusted other in your life to do together— is an excellent one. Try to make doing it fun. Laugh at yourselves and cry for yourselves, and talk, share and learn together how you can make your relationship more vital, less hurtful and more fulfilling. The Letter(s) done together will add a whole new dimension to what you have to talk about. And this talk will enrich your relationships and your lives.

The fourth option is also an excellent one and is my personal favorite. It is for you as a boss (or as a parent) to use the Letter(s) as a basis for building your team. The process for doing this is described at the beginning of this Letter. There are at least four benefits to the team members:

First, when they find that you, the boss, have given them permission to share some of their feelings with you, they will become more trusting. They will start trusting and talking with each other. The climate of your team will start changing to become a warmer, more open, more caring place to work and live.

Second, there will be some carryover effect with individual team members' families. There will be a societal benefit from what you have started.

Third, it will make your work-team become more effective. Old hurts will be cured. Old misunderstandings will be cleared up. You will get more data on how to make the work move better and quicker. The members will gradually move from a basic motivation of a narrow self-interest, "what's in it for me?," to a more enlightened self-interest, "What can I do that will help the whole team?"

How long will it take for a team to discuss a Letter? The Letters come out every two months. This means one Letter to deal with in every 320 hours of work. Could you possibly spare 1/2 of 1% of that time to build your team? Could you somehow find 12 hours each 2 months? I'll wager that no matter how busy you are or how much pressure there is on production that more than this much time is wasted *each week!* So find the time—and start the process! The only real down-side risk is that nothing happens, that people won't talk. And if this is the case, you can be absolutely sure that you really do have a problem. You can't lose!
Good luck.

Bill Crockett

THE HUMAN RELATIONS LETTER
Dedicated to the Art of Creating Effective Relationships

Issue #16

SELF-INTEREST
Our organizations will not be profitable nor strong if they are only held together by the rotten rope of self interest .

1 **Introduction**

The principal force that motivates all humanity is self-interest. The world will always be governed by it. The wise man, understanding this, will find ways to make it serve his own needs, hopefully good ones!

The statement above is a sad but true commentary on the world of men. Religion, laws and social sanctions have not been able, over the centuries, to stamp out this powerful interest in "self." If we wish to be effective leaders, managers, politicians, husbands, wives, parents— people, we will first recognize the pervasive power of self-interest and then deport ourselves in ways that enable us and the causes we represent to join with and flow with this powerful human tide. To buck it or to try to deflect it is sheer folly because, in the end, we will fail. So how do we cause this powerful force to enhance the welfare of our organizations?

1 **Kinds of Self-Interest**

The first kind of self-interest is the narrow kind—me! I am at the center of my universe and I want that universe to serve me first and foremost. I care little about the problems of you out there or the problems that I cause you by my serving me.

I will water my lawn even if there is a water shortage. I will burn logs in my fireplace even if it pollutes the air. I will use sprays even though it may endanger the ozone layer. My personal gratification is my only concern.

Akin to this narrow self-interest is our demand for immediate gratification vs. our long-term best interest. I want it *now*. I will do it *now*. I will risk the future! If I smoke, I might get cancer, but it may not happen to me!

— I will risk breaking the law to get rich (Keating, Milken, Bosky)!

— I will risk AIDS for quick sexual gratification.

— The destruction of the rain forests? Oh, who needs to worry about that now!

— Diet? Exercise? Save? Recycle? Get an education? Take out insurance? Work? All of these and many, many more impinge on our immediate self-interest, so "don't worry about them." Let the future take care of itself. *Now* is the moment for me.

It is the view of some financial and organizational analysts that one of the chief weaknesses of our modern corporate management is their emphasis on short-term results vs. building for the future, as the Japanese tend to do.

Second, there is what might be called enlightened self-interest. This means that, by some process, I do take a slightly larger long-term interest in something. There is something I should think about and perhaps do something about now, because I can see that there will be a future payoff for me.

Yes, maybe I should attend the PTA, for it might help my child with the school and teacher.

Yes, I will join. Yes, I will give. Yes, I will speak. Yes, I will serve. And on and on. There are literally thousands of ways that we can become involved because of our own enlightened self-interest . And only we know how each may serve us.

Then there is what might be called "group" or "team self-interest." The person's personal identity becomes that of the group and his self-interest is served when the self-interest of the group is served. We see this kind of self-interest evidenced in sports teams, in families, and on rare occasions, in work teams. This also is the motivating force that causes street gangs to flourish in our cities. Belonging to such groups increases people's feelings of potency and uniquely serves their self-interest.

Finally, there is what might be called "our national self-interest." This is the interest we have in what our government does to us, requires of us, wants from us, hopes for us, etc. This is quite a remote interest for most of us. Oh, to be sure, we bitch, moan and groan—"Ain't it awful"— and then don't write our representatives, don't attend meetings and don't vote.

The differences in our degree of national self-interest was vividly portrayed to all of us by our recent involvement in two armed conflicts—Vietnam and the Persian Gulf. In the former, there was little feeling of national interest. Young people by the thousands avoided serving. "Hell no, I won't go" became their cry. Contrast this with the Persian Gulf conflict. The nation, for one brief moment, rallied behind our government's decision in an outburst of national self-interest.

What was the difference in the two situations? What caused the difference?

- ## The Magic Force of Positive Self-Interest

The ingredient that was missing in our people during the Vietnam conflict and was present in the Gulf was a strong emotional commitment. In order to have an enlarged self-interest—beyond our own narrow boundaries—there must be a strong emotional underpinning. This emotional underpinning sparks a broadened self-interest and sustains it.

The Japanese attack on Pearl Harbor galvanized our nation into an emotional frenzy of national self-interest.

The continued brutal treatment inflicted on our prisoners of war kept people's emotions high. There was no letup in our national self-interest. As a consequence, the greater national interest overcame narrow self-interest, and people volunteered for all kinds of work, including joining the armed forces and risking the sacrifice of life itself. Of course Hitler used the same tactics to galvanize the German people into starting World War II.

The lesson from these examples is one that all of us who have the responsibility of managing people should not only take to heart but put into daily use.

- ## The Source of Conflict

One of the chief sources of conflict in the world is that of competing self-interests. I want one thing and you want the same thing, while there is only enough for one of us. If I am your boss or your parent or some other authority figure, I may be able to force you to do what I want and thus deny the satisfaction of your self-interest. Often when this happens, you may be able, even in your weak position, to do things for revenge that will subtly sabotage my endeavor. Then when I don't accomplish my objectives because of what seems to be your poor attitude, your lackluster performance or your poor motivation, I become angry and more punishing to you. "You will do it!" And so it goes, with the relationship becoming ever more strained and toxic.

This downward progression happens in families. It happens in organizations. It happens in government (witness the anger that the public feels about politicians in general). It happens between bosses and their subordinates. And whenever and wherever it happens, the positive emotions of the relationship vanish and are replaced by the negatives of fear, anger and reprisal. Powerful self-interest have prevailed.

In most organizations, the prevailing management style has been strongly authoritarian with the "Do-as-I-say" boss imposing his self-interest upon his subordinates. Modern management theory suggests that a more collaborative style may achieve better results because the self-interest of the subordinates become of more concern to this kind of a manager.

● **The Business World**
The business world has long floundered in considering the question, "How can we motivate our people, both the white-collar managerial group as well as the blue-collar workers to achieve great results?" About all they have come up with is a basket full of financial perks.

The business world has also been intrigued with how and why the Japanese management system does so well. One answer may be the high degree of emotional commitment that the Japanese system seems to generate and to sustain. IBM used to have some of this kind of personal enthusiasm.

In the old days under the founder, Thomas Watson, there was a high degree of positive emotionalism in the work force. A sale was cause for celebration. A bell was rung and the whole team celebrated. At meetings, songs were sung about the company; and everyone celebrated IBM's success. It was not just perks and pay. It was people's enthusiastic behavior that helped to create a corporate atmosphere (climate) that transferred narrow self-interest into a broader company interest that was the old IBM.

I hasten to admit that I have no hard data to support this contention; but when organizations lose their positive human emotional qualities and become just big, bureaucratic, humdrum business-as-usual legal entities, people then can easily revert to their old narrow self-interest selves. As a manager of a Fortune 500 company recently told a reporter who asked him why he didn't opt for the company's lucrative early retirement plan, "Why should I retire? I get $90,000 pay with lots of perks and I leave the office at 3 p.m. each day and no one seems to care"! In such a climate there is no larger, extended self-interest.

● **The Dreadful Cost of Self-Interest**
Self-interest is narrow and selfish. It is deeply fortified by memories of past injustices or by fear of the future and the present. It nurses its hurts and its imagined injustices. It is a fortress mentality. It is so deeply fortified by strong emotions that logic has little effect and facts have little value. It is one of the most powerful and most pervasive of all the emotional forces that afflict mankind. It is a holdover from the caveman

period when survival was based on self-interest. But it has no place in civilized relationships.

One of the dreadful outcomes of rampant self-interest is the heinous acts of violence and destruction that are justified in its name. This includes hostage-taking, outright murder, and the increasing tensions between ethnic groups, business and labor, etc. The forces of self-interest are evil and are destructive for society as a whole.

Given the destructive nature of "justified" self-interest, it behooves people to become aware of its sources. When people in their relationships with each other act only out of their own narrow self-interest, they set up an adversarial climate that breeds the negative emotions which motivate the actions that cause the situation to further deteriorate. These actions will then very effectively dry up collaboration for the common good and will cause all communication to stop. Classic examples of this in action is the long-standing stalemate in the Middle East between Israel and its Arab neighbors, and the morbid state of the social, economic, and political affairs in this country.

In the context of our organizational structures, it is especially important for all of us to be very careful of how we handle our relationships with our bosses as well as with our subordinates so that our behavior reflects the more productive and effective motivation, i.e., mutual self-interest.

● **The Challenge for Managers—Creating the Magic**

It seems to me that the challenge for business, for managers, and for any of us who exercise power and authority over people is to help them—cause them to enlarge the scope of their self-interest. It means helping them create a vision of opportunity. It means helping them to create a work climate that is challenging and inspiring.This means helping them to become emotionally enthusiastic and committed to a common cause. It is this human emotional ingredient that is the magic that causes the difference!

● **How Is It Done?**

If I really, absolutely and for sure knew the answer, I would be rich. I would have the world of business beating a path to the door of my consulting business. But I have some experience and some ideas that have worked for me.

— First and foremost, the climate of the work group—and better yet, the whole organization—must be one that is good for people if the company is to have the broadened self-interest of the worker. Almost any worker, from the bottom to the top of an organization, can make a list of qualities that will make the work place a good people place.I asked a randomly-selected group of managers to define such a climate. They quickly listed such things as mutual concern, mutual trust, mutual support, mutual respect, fun, involvement, commitment, and freedom from fear and reprisal.

— Second, the managers—the whole organization—must wholeheartedly believe that such a climate is not only good for people but that it will also be good for the managers, for the organization, and for the clients as well. This means adopting a management style that is more collaborative and less authoritarian in nature. It means treating people in humane, considerate ways.

—Third, the managers—the whole organization—must be willing to commit some time each and every week to the task of building these qualities into their work teams. This is called "Team Building." One way of doing this is to use these *Human Relations Letters* as a starting place. Have the team members read one of the Letters, then set aside an hour each to talk about the realities of the Letter in the context of the team, here and now. It will be slow at first. People will be quiet or angry or resistive. But patience will pay off. The end that you want to achieve is to empower the team members to talk honestly about their feelings and the situations that motivate them and help create their ideas for improvement. All that you, the manager, has to do is to hold your tongue and your temper, listen, ask questions for understanding, be honest if you can't do or get done what they suggest, have patience, make action plans, celebrate breakthroughs and keep your eye on the goal—"A place that is good for people." When you have achieved this goal, you will have turned loose the magic of achieving broadened self-interest.

— Fourth, the team managers—the whole organization—must not expect quick results. Miracles won't happen overnight. This is not a quick fix kind of remedy. It will take some time to cause team members to really trust, to be open and to behave in the new ways that the new climate requires. There will be people who can't (won't) change. There will be managers who say that it's too tough to manage in this way—that the old "tell them" style was easier, simpler and quicker. It will take patience and perseverance on the part of all who believe.

● **Conclusion**
Many theories exist and much has been written about the manager's responsibility to positively motivate their subordinates so that work-goals can be reached; but very little has been written about the responsibilities of followership.

I believe that all organizations, even society itself, are shortchanging themselves by not having learning programs and seminars that teach people in all walks of life the responsibilities of positive followership. And the first and foremost quality that should be taught and practiced and emphasized and rewarded is the primacy of the leader-manager's self-interest in the relationship. So long as the organization's treatment of people is fair and so long as the style of the boss is not overly harsh or brutal, it is the duty of followers at all levels to put the self-interest of the boss (the organization) above their own.

When this occurs in our organizations, there may be a revival of enthusiasm, an increase in positive attitudes, a renewed motivation, and the emergence of helpful collaboration that will make American management once again the world standard.

Yes, enthusiastic followership that sublimates personal self-interest for the good of the whole is a key ingredient of organization success.

Bill Crockett

● **Questions for Discussion**

One of the best ways for a work-team to further study and discuss the concept of followership is to use the book, "The Secrets of a Dynamic Subordinate That Every Manager Should Know." It is available in bookstores, or if you prefer, through CABS (Fax 602-538-0955 or Telephone 602-972-4925).

Index

Administrator of Security and Consular Affairs: 25, 26
Africa: 76
AID: 103
Andrews Air Force Base: 61
Assistant Secretary of State: 76
Assistant Secretary for Administration: 103
Ball: 27, 66
Baptista: 35
Barrett: 103
Bill (Crockett): 25, 26, 29, 60, 69, 70, 73, 74, 76, 82, 87, 88, 96, 97, 98, 99, 100, 103, 104
Boston: 71, 74
Bowles: 25
Budget and Accounting Officer: 76
Bush, President: 68
Carter, President Jimmy: 123
Castro: 26, 35
CBS News: 18
CCPS: 103, 104
Chiang Kai-shek: 35
Chief of Police (Phoenix): 77
China: 35
Churchill: 123
City Manager: 77
Coast Guard: 32
Communist: 35, 71
Congress: 34, 35, 36, 76
Contra: 95
Crockett (Robert): 111
Crockett (Verla): 114
Crockett (William): 36, 101, 103, 104
Dakar: 52
Department of State: 103, 111
Deputy Under Secretary: 25, 27, 34, 66, 88, 95, 96, 99, 102, 104, 111
Dwinell: 76
Eisenhower Administration: 35
Erhlichmann: 29
Exxon Valdez: 31, 32, 66
FBI: 36
Fifi: 15, 19
Foreign Affairs Committee: 69
Foreign Relations Committee: 75
Foreign Service Officer: 35
Governor of New Hampshire: 76

Halderman: 29
Hammer: 123
Harr: 103
Hubbard: 29
HUD: 32
IBM: 37, 38
Internal Security Subcommittee: 35, 36
Ioccoca: 17, 21
Iran/Contra: 38
IRS: 32
Japan: 66
Johnson (President): 4, 25, 26, 27, 69, 70, 72, 73, 76
Johnson (Vice President): 28, 43, 52, 53, 60, 61, 85, 86
Keating: 20
Keating Five: 20
Kellogg Company: 91
Kennedy Administartion: 35
Kennedy, President: 23, 25, 51, 54, 89, 96, 111
Kennedy (Robert): 23
LaMonte: 92
LBJ: 123
Mama and Papa: 72, 73, 74, 75
Mansfield: 5
Maslow: 14, 44
McArthur, General: 17, 21, 92
McCarthy: 35, 36
McFarland: 94
Milken: 20
Mosher: 103
Naples: 71
NATO: 71
Newsweek: 123
Nixon, President: 29
North: 20, 28, 38, 94
Office of Security: 66
Pakistan: 61
Peters: 102
Poindexter: 20, 28, 94
Reagan White House: 28
Reagan, President: 29
Regan: 29
Rooney: 52, 53
Rowan: 5
Rusk: 25, 26, 27, 34, 35, 37, 47, 60, 66, 74, 75, 85, 90, 95, 96, 98, 99, 102, 104

Schartzkopf: 68
Senegal: 52, 53
Security People: 71
Sicily: 69, 71
State Department: 24, 34, 35, 60, 70, 76, 103, 105
Sununu: 29
T-Group: 114
Thatcher: 12, 123
Tylenol: 66
UN Force: 92
U.S. Foreign Service: 35
United States: 71
U.S. Consul General: 72
U.S. Immigration Service: 71
U.S. Military: 71
U.S. Senate: 34, 36
Vietnam: 27, 37, 70
Visa Office: 66
Wall Street Journal: 91
White House: 70
White House Staff: 48
World Trade Sales Convention: 38
WW II: 37

Order Form

☎ **Telephone orders:** Call (602) 972-4925

✳ **Fax orders:**   (602) 583-0955

✉ **Postal Orders:** Center for Applied Behavioral Sciences
P.O. Box 1639
Sun City, AZ 85372

Please send _____ copies of *The Secrets of a Dynamic Subordinate That Every Manager Should Know* **at $21.95 each. I understand that I may return any books for a full refund—for any reason, no questions asked.**

❑ Please send a free copy of the CABS Human Relations Letter.

❑ Please send a free brochure on the Leadership/Management Development seminar.

❑ Please send a free brochure on the Work Team Development seminar.

Company name:_____

Name:_____

Address:_____

City:_____

Sales tax:
Please add 5.5% for books shipped to Arizona addresses.

Packing and shipping charges:
Book Rate: $2.00 for the first book and 75 cents for each additional book.
(Surface shipping may take three to four weeks.)
Air Mail: $3.50 per book.

Payment:
❑ Check   ❑ Money Order

IMPORTANT NOTE: Please call the publisher for applicable discounts on all orders of 10 or more books.

Order Form

☎ **Telephone orders:** Call (602) 972-4925

✳ **Fax orders:** (602) 583-0955

✉ **Postal Orders:** Center for Applied Behavioral Sciences
P.O. Box 1639
Sun City, AZ 85372

Please send _____ copies of *The Secrets of a Dynamic Subordinate That Every Manager Should Know* at $21.95 each. I understand that I may return any books for a full refund—for any reason, no questions asked.

❏ Please send a free copy of the CABS Human Relations Letter.

❏ Please send a free brochure on the Leadership/Management Development seminar.

❏ Please send a free brochure on the Work Team Development seminar.

Company name:_____

Name:_____

Address:_____

City:_____

Sales tax:
Please add 5.5% for books shipped to Arizona addresses.

Packing and shipping charges:
Book Rate: $2.00 for the first book and 75 cents for each additional book.
(Surface shipping may take three to four weeks.)
Air Mail: $3.50 per book.

Payment:
❏ Check   ❏ Money Order

IMPORTANT NOTE: Please call the publisher for applicable discounts on all orders of 10 or more books.